CHRISTOPHER NICHOLSON

CHRISTOPHER NICHOLSON

NEIL BINGHAM

A.D. ACADEMY EDITIONS

ACKNOWLEDGEMENTS

Dedicated to Jonathan Hoyle

Published in collaboration with the Royal Institute of British Architects.
All illustrative material is from the British Architectural Library, Drawings and Photographs Collections,
Royal Institute of British Architects, unless otherwise stated. The images on p8, p104, p105 (above) and p106 (above) are
reproduced courtesy of *The Architectural Review*. The image on p105 (below) is reproduced courtesy of the
National Monuments Record.

SERIES EDITOR: Jill Lever
From an original idea by Stuart Durant

FRONT COVER: Axonometric of the bar, London Gliding Club, Dunstable, 1936 (plate 39)
BACK COVER: Design for the studio, Fryern Court, Hampshire, for Augustus John, c1934 (plate 12)
PAGE 2: Christopher Nicholson at home at 29 Paultons Square, London, c1937 (photographed by John Somerset Murray)

Published in Great Britain in 1996 by
ACADEMY EDITIONS
an imprint of

ACADEMY GROUP LTD
42 Leinster Gardens, London W2 3AN
Member of VCH PUBLISHING GROUP

ISBN: 1 85490 445 0

Distributed to the trade in the USA by
NATIONAL BOOK NETWORK, INC
4720 Boston Way, Lanham, Maryland 20706

Printed and bound in Singapore

CONTENTS

FOREWORD

The first of Christopher 'Kit' Nicholson's drawings came to the RIBA in 1967; a dozen sheets of designs and details for his eclectically Modern studio for Augustus John, given by Sir Hugh Casson, Nicholson's colleague and friend. And it was Casson, twenty-two years later, who suggested to Nicholson's widow, EQ, and her architect-turned-painter son, Tim, that more drawings might be given to the RIBA.

After Christopher Nicholson's office at 110 Brompton Road was closed, his drawings were transferred to the family's home at Yew Cottage, near Cranborne, Dorset, where they were kept in the ping-pong shed, having been taken out of their original cardboard tubes with the job number stencilled on the lid. When the mice began to damage the drawings, Tim Nicholson re-housed them in a plan-chest in the drawing room before bringing them up to his London house in the early 1970s. With the utmost generosity, EQ and Tim Nicholson agreed to present the RIBA with all the surviving drawings – about 1,100 – as well as record books and photographs.

In January 1990, the drawings were collected and the task of flattening and initial preservation was done by Siân Williams while Neil Bingham undertook the research, sorting and cataloguing. He was much helped by lists of works and a copy of Tim Nicholson's Thames Polytechnic thesis on his father's pre-war career, and in identifying and attributing the various schemes by both Tim Nicholson and Sir Hugh Casson.

EQ Nicholson (born 1908) died on 7 September 1992 having lived long enough to enjoy a revival of interest in her work as a designer and artist. Christopher Nicholson's career, interrupted by war and ended by a fatal accident, was a short one, but it spanned an important period, 1927 to 1948, and reflected the opportunities offered by an artistically influential milieu as well as the sense of freshness and adventure that informs his work.

I am most grateful to Dr Neil Bingham, Assistant Curator of the RIBA Drawings Collection, for agreeing to write this, the fourth of a new series of monograph books from the Drawings Collection of the Royal Institute of British Architects.

Jill Lever (Series editor of the RIBA Drawings Monographs)

AN APPRECIATION BY SIR HUGH CASSON

Appropriately enough, the first person I met when I arrived at the Cambridge School of Architecture at 9.30 on the first morning of term turned out to be not – as I thought – a rather mature student but our First Year Tutor – Christopher Nicholson.

With a high forehead from which black curly hair was brushed back into a cantilever shape fitting over his collar, he was wearing horn-rim spectacles and armed with a smile of welcome. He had arrived from an American university school of architecture as our Year Tutor. He seemed to like the look of us and we returned the compliment immediately and with genuine pleasure. We all took to him at once and he remained for all of us that year a true friend and adviser, helpful always with simple advice. Our first design problem was a classical little gazebo for the centre of Great Court at Trinity College which involved a compulsory visit to the college in the lunch hour.

We had several visits from his elegant father, Sir William, and occasionally his painter brother Ben. Christopher and his wife lived opposite the school, working from his upstairs office. We missed him when we passed on to the Bartlett School of Architecture in London for completion of our training.

The news of his death in a glider crash was a serious blow to us all. I was lucky to have been offered a place in his London office where I worked till war broke out and for a short time afterwards. A fine teacher, a cheerful companion, a beautiful draughtsman like all the family, and a splendid and helpful teacher, he is remembered by all of his students with great affection and gratitude.

Hugh Casson in the Nicholson office at 110 Brompton Road, London, c1947

The London Gliding Club, Dunstable, Bedfordshire, with a Falcon III sailplane emerging from the hangar, 1936
(photographed by Dell & Wainwright)

PREFACE

While researching 1930s British airport buildings for a lecture in 1990, I visited the London Gliding Club near Dunstable. This was my first introduction to Christopher Nicholson's architecture, and I had the joy of not only touring its almost untouched interior, but gliding over it in a sailplane. It is a beautiful object from the air, a sensuous white shape set in the deep green dip of the Downs. In the glider, as I quietly and gently floated through space, with a panoramic view – for as the passenger I was placed disconcertingly in the nose of the plane with the pilot behind – I found myself struck by how buildings seen from above take on different architectural characteristics than when observed from the usual earthbound perspective. Consequently, when I came to better understand Nicholson's architecture, I realised that one of the major reasons such buildings as his Gliding Club, Augustus John's studio, and Kit's Close were designed sculpturally was because Nicholson, as a pilot, instinctively visualised buildings in the round, all sides and plan simultaneously.

This ability of Christopher Nicholson, a brilliant young architect of early British Modernism, to conceive buildings in new forms is reflected in the development of his draughtsmanship. That we are able to study this development of style is due to the preservation of his architectural drawings by his son, Mr Tim Nicholson. I am overwhelmingly in Tim Nicholson's debt. He has so generously shared his knowledge about his father and family with me, and helped me understand through his own kind nature, the deeply felt love for art that has enlivened three generations of Nicholsons.

Tim Nicholson also put me in touch with many of his father's colleagues, clients and friends, who shared their memories with me, and whom I would like to thank: Mrs Eliza Banks, Sir Thomas Bazley, Mrs Susan Carr, Mr Neville Conder, Miss Mary Fedden, Mrs Deenagh Goold-Adams, Sir Leslie Martin, Mrs Ursula Mommens, Mrs Aurea Morshead and Mrs Vanessa Winchester. I would particularly like to express my appreciation to Sir Hugh Casson, whose recollections, because he and Nicholson were such close friends and worked together, have been invaluable. I would also like to acknowledge those people who have given me information and assistance: Mr David Burgess-Wise, Mrs Jill Claiden, Ms Cathy Courtney, Mr Jim Forster, Mr Keith Hayward, Lieutenant Colonel N McKnight, Dr Alan Powers, Mr Derek Samson, Mr Nigel Tallis, Mr Xavier Guzman Urbiola, Mr Antony Walker, Mr Christopher Wilk and Mrs Carola Zogolovitch. To Mr Andy Smart and Miss Karen Bengall of AC Cooper Ltd, my thanks for their careful photography; and to Miss Maggie Toy, Mr Andrea Bettella and Miss Ellie Duffy of Academy Editions, my appreciation for their meticulous preparation of this book.

And finally, I would like to thank my colleagues at the RIBA Drawings Collection: Miss Eleanor Gawne, Mr Tim Knox, Mr Jonathan Makepeace, Mr Andrew Norris, Mrs Charlotte Podro, Miss Siân Williams, and especially, Mrs Jill Lever, our former Curator, who guided us so wisely over the years and kindly asked me to write this book.

Neil Bingham

Christopher Nicholson in the photographer's studio he designed for John Somerset Murray, 144A Sloane Street, London, c1935
(photographed by John Somerset Murray)

INTRODUCTION

The geometrics which had interested me so much exclusively before, I now felt were bleak and empty. **They wanted filling.** *They were still as much present to my mind as ever, but submerged in the coloured vegetation, the flesh and blood, that is life . . .* [1]

Wyndham Lewis

Christopher David George Nicholson, known to his family and friends simply as Kit, died at the age of forty-four in a small chapel on a mountain side in Italy. During the afternoon of 28 July 1948, he had set out in his Slingsby Gull sailplane from the little airfield of Samadan in Switzerland on the eighth day of the International Gliding Championship. Nicholson was one of the five members of the British team. Flying through the Maloja Pass, Kit soared high over the mountains above Lake Como. Unknown to him, his team-mate Donald Greig had hit an overhead cable on the other side of the same mountain and had been killed. Nicholson, an experienced pilot, must suddenly have been enveloped in cloud, which had grown from below in the damp air, blinding him. Pulling up hard, he stalled on top of the mountain. Remarkably, Nicholson was in little pain and, apparently, not seriously injured. Shepherds found him and began to carry him down in a slow descent. As light faded, they reached a little chapel at 3,000 feet where they found a Catholic priest.

Nicholson's wife, who was waiting for news at the hospital, was to write to her husband's brother, the artist Ben Nicholson, and relate that the priest had been 'a charming and intelligent person and was a great comfort to Kit' as they chatted together in French. But,

suddenly, Nicholson died of internal injuries. 'Cheerful and confident till the end. I'm convinced he didn't know at all that he was going to die.'[2]

Christopher Nicholson's ashes were scattered over the Marlborough Downs, released into the air high overhead by his friend, the pioneering woman glider Ann Welch.

Nicholson's untimely death ended a short architectural life. Nevertheless, as the drawings in this book illustrate so well, it was a concentrated but brilliant career which had begun in the late twenties, blossomed around 1933, was interrupted in 1939 by six years of war, and then ended with a brief but energetic few years after demobilization. In all, he practised for just over ten years. It is somewhat futile to speculate how Nicholson's architecture and office would have developed had he lived, but at the time of his death he was an established figure in the worlds of architecture and industrial design. No doubt a comfortable future awaited him, and with all his connections, he surely would have been involved with the 1951 Festival of Britain. As it is, Christopher Nicholson's reputation remains historically solid, resting upon a group of major buildings from the early Modern period in Britain, notably Augustus John's studio, the London Gliding Club, Monkton House and Kit's Close.

The Nicholson office, although dissolved after Christopher's death, continued in spirit through Hugh Casson, who had joined Nicholson in 1935 on a full-time basis. Just two weeks before Nicholson suffered his fatal accident, Casson wrote to him saying that he had signed up as the Director of Architecture for the

1951 Festival of Britain.[3] Sir Hugh, knighted for his Festival responsibilities, has always assumed a modest role in Nicholson's architectural and design work, insisting that he merely carried out Nicholson's original ideas. But the architectural drawings that have survived from the office show that Casson was a major force in Nicholson's office, perhaps not always in the early design stages of a project, but certainly in the finished drawings. Casson's perspectives are especially lively and seductive, the perfect bait for capturing clients and clinching commissions. They are as personable as the man himself. Illustrations by Hugh Casson are strongly represented on the following pages, not because they form the majority of the surviving drawings but because they are often the most visually stimulating.

Nicholson's own skills and artistry in drawing were considerable. 'Kit was a beautiful and quick draughtsman,' Casson recalls, 'and a decisive designer'.[4] Christopher came from a family of artists, was surrounded by artists, and had wanted to be an artist. The experimentation in his architecture resulted not only from the stimulus he received from talking with and seeing the work of other progressive architects, but also from living with avant-garde painters and sculptors. The twenties and thirties were lively decades for Modern art, and the strongest stylistic movements which shot through the English art world often found their parallel in Nicholson's architectural drawings, and consequently his architecture. His family, and especially his brother Ben, the internationally respected abstract painter, had an immense influence on his work. And, no doubt, the reverse was true. Their artistic circle, infused with an optimistic passion for a rational and mechanised world, saw Christopher Nicholson as the epitome of the new Modernism.

Christopher Nicholson was the youngest child in his family, born on 16 December 1904 at 1 Pilgrim's Lane, Hampstead, London. Both his parents were painters. His father was William Nicholson who had trained at the school of art in Bushey run by Sir Hubert von Herkomer, and then in Paris, at the Académie Julian. William had established his reputation in the 1890s with a series of posters which he executed with his brother-in-law, James Pryde. He was a popular, gregarious and dapper figure, like his elderly mentor, James McNeill Whistler. His most famous and well-known work from this period was the affectionate silhouette-portrait of Queen Victoria. In the year Christopher was born, William was working on the costumes for JM Barrie's new play, *Peter Pan*. Later, he began to paint landscapes and still-lives with luminous paint qualities which impart a haunting clarity to the subjects. He was also in great demand as a portrait painter.

William Nicholson married Mabel Pryde in 1893. Occupied by a growing family, she had less time to pursue her painting career. Ben had been born in 1894, Anthony in 1897 and Nancy in 1899. Mabel did manage to work at home, and her double portrait of Nancy and Christopher in the family's home at The Grange, Rottingdean, Sussex, with its dappled light and domestic mysteriousness, captures the serenity of a seventeenth century Dutch genre painting.

As a child, Christopher was surrounded by the literary, artistic and theatrical stars of Edwardian society. Ellen Terry, Max Beerbohm and Rudyard Kipling are just a few names from his parents' circle of friends. Holidays were spent in Paris, and Dieppe, the fashionable seaside resort of painters. William Orpen painted a group portrait of the whole family, finished in 1908 and titled *A Bloomsbury Family*. William Nicholson is seated in the foreground with the young Christopher who is wearing a burgundy high-bodiced baby's dress and childishly pointing at his father.[5]

In 1917, the Nicholsons moved to 11 Apple Tree Yard, St James's, London. Their near neighbour was one of William's most intimate friends, Edwin Lutyens, who had his office at No.7.

A double tragedy struck the family in 1918 when first Christopher's mother died in July during the great influenza epidemic, and then his brother Anthony succumbed to wounds on the battlefield in France in October. The following year, William married the wealthy Edith Stuart Wortley, an arrangement which allowed them to purchase The Manor in Sutton Veny, Wiltshire, in 1923, where Christopher was to spend many of his holidays.

Meanwhile, from about 1916, Christopher had been attending Heddon Court preparatory school in East Barnet, north London. In 1919 he was accepted at Gresham's School, a progressive establishment near Holt, Norfolk. Among his fellow pupils were the poet WH Auden, the actor Donald Wolfit and Erskine Childers, later President of the Irish Republic. In Christopher's house was James M Richards, subsequently the influential architectural critic and editor of *The Architectural Review*. The two of them did not become good friends until the thirties.[6]

Nicholson, always a keen sportsman, was in the swimming and rugby football teams, and captained both hockey and cricket. Tennis was another passion, and later at university he played for his college. When he was in his late twenties, he and his brother Ben, along with their friend the artist Adrian Stokes, went so far as to invent a new form of table tennis which they tried to get Slazenger to market.[7]

At first, wary of perpetuating the Nicholson tradition of being a painter, Christopher went up to Jesus College, Cambridge in 1923 to study English literature. But he very soon switched to the School of Architecture, where he could give full reign to his love of art but also satisfy his pragmatic nature. He spent three years at Cambridge, following the established course which advocated a practical grounding in the classical orders, the English grand manner of such giants as Wren, and the more low-key vernacular tradition of Norman Shaw and WR

Lethaby. His architectural education was an outcome of the twenties inheritance of a powerful Edwardian classicism and the stimulating Arts and Crafts movement which had dominated architectural practice before the First World War. Edwin Lutyens stood firmly in both these camps; and Nicholson, who admired and emulated him, was also personally encouraged by him to find his own feet in this comfortably British world which felt it had no rivals.

However, the winds of change were blowing, and they were just beginning to reach Britain's unbreached shores. At Cambridge, Nicholson dutifully carried out his assignments to design mausoleums and clock towers, listened to the ramblings of that rather eccentric practitioner of the Arts and Crafts, ES Prior, and developed a fine architectural draughtsmanship. Meanwhile, younger teachers like George Checkley and Harold Tomlinson were catching on to new developments, especially what was happening on the Continent, and Nicholson formed a great sympathy with them.

Ben would come to visit, bringing with him electrifying and first-hand knowledge of the latest trends in the arts. In November 1925, for example, Ben descended on Christopher and, no doubt with his student-brother in tow, swept off to the Fitzwilliam Museum to look at works by the Primitive painters.[8] The following month Ben was scheduled to exhibit five paintings in a Paris show alongside works by Brancusi, Delauney, Léger, Miró, Mondrian, Ozenfant and Picasso.

As Christopher was a decade younger than his brother, it took time for him to catch up with Ben's search for a more disciplined and simplified style. Hence, for the 1926 staging of *Edward II* by the Cambridge Marlowe Society, Christopher designed the costumes and sets and painted the backdrop in a style reminiscent of one of his father's early woodcuts.

A year spent in the United States also reinforced his classical training rather than spurring him on to new developments; between September 1926 and June 1927, Nicholson studied architecture at Princeton University on a Davison Scholarship. In common with all American schools of architecture, the course at Princeton was run on Beaux Arts principles. Nicholson created large drawings, usually in the classical style and always with complex planning. None of the finished drawings from his student years at Cambridge or Princeton has survived, although a set of glass negatives of some of his American projects – designs for a manor house, a ballroom, and a municipal observatory (plate 1) – illustrates Nicholson's superb draughtsmanship. This Beaux Arts training, with its emphasis upon symmetry, especially in plan, appealed to Nicholson's sense of order and strengthened the foundation for his later experiments in mathematical proportioning.

Upon his return to England, Nicholson spent much of his time sketching, reading and staying at Banks Head, the farm cottage in Cumberland acquired by Ben and his wife, the painter Winifred Roberts. Christopher had previously visited Ben and Winifred in their Italian villa overlooking Lake Lugano, which the couple lived in intermittently over a period of two years following their marriage in 1920. Winifred and Christopher got along well together. She painted his portrait about this time in which he is seated reading a book, its rose-coloured binding a block of brightness against his white sweater.

Winifred's parents lived not far from Banks Head, at Boothby, a large house near the town of Brampton. Her father was Charles Roberts and her mother Lady Cecilia, daughter of George Howard, 9th Earl of Carlisle. The Roberts' were to be Christopher's first clients, and set the pattern for almost all his commissions, which came through family and friends. Nicholson did two jobs for them, the first a garden house in the grounds of Boothby (plate 2) and the second the Carlisle Memorial seat at Brampton (plate 3). His stylistic sources are obvious: the local vernacular buildings which fill his

sketchbooks of the period, and Lutyens. Neither building would have looked out of place in one of the Cumberland landscapes which Ben and Winifred were painting at the time.

In February 1929, Nicholson returned to Cambridge to stay with his former tutor Harold Tomlinson, to help him prepare competition designs for a local cinema. He was soon angling for a teaching position in his old school of architecture which he hoped would progress to an eight-year instructorship. As it happened, he began teaching first-year students in April, and only remained for about two years. One of his students during this time was Hugh Casson.

It was an immensely stimulating period, one in which Nicholson started to absorb the new style coming from abroad and to see the early results of its stark architectural vocabulary as a few examples began to be built in England. At first he was dubious of becoming fully committed, and like many burgeoning Modernists, believed in the harmony of old and new. In his diary for 19 March 1929, he wrote:

> My cinema elevation has for its stone base a crib of a group of exits to Easton and Robertson's Horticultural Hall in Westminster. Above in brick is a double row of five sash windows with the central two arcaded. The whole is topped by a deep stone coping. A rather unsuccessful attempt to do something modern (horrible expression) and yet in tone with the Georgian atmosphere of the market place.

But he was soon buying the most advanced architectural books by pioneering moderns like Bruno Taut, André Lurçat, Le Corbusier and Richard Neutra. Through Tomlinson he met the great arbiter of modern taste in Cambridge, Manny Forbes, who had just had his house Finella rebuilt and decorated by his protégé, Raymond McGrath. By May 1930, Nicholson had been to Paris. In a letter to Ben, who had just returned from organising his forthcoming show, Christopher writes like an enthusiastic convert:

> Have you seen any Corbusian stuff (perhaps those in the Square Docteur Blanche) and if so what do you think of them? I thought his stuff ever so much better than Mallet-Stevens. Apart from the whiteness and obvious concern with proportion I thought M.S. second rate.[9]

At Cambridge, Nicholson met EQ Myers and they married in December 1931. Lively, outspoken, a talented fabric printer and designer, EQ was a natural addition to the free-spirited Nicholson family. Before they met, she had studied textile design in Paris for a time, and had worked in London for Marion Dorn. They collaborated on several projects, and she often helped out in the office for a few hours a day. She found an ally in Christopher's sister, Nancy, who by 1930 had separated from her husband, the poet and author Robert Graves, and set up Poulk Prints.

In the years following Cambridge, between 1931 and 1933, Nicholson found modest designing jobs through family. His two main clients were Sir Thomas Bazley, a cousin of Ben's wife Winifred,[10] and Richard Blennerhassett, who was EQ's uncle by marriage.[11] His most architectural work was converting a conservatory at Sir Thomas's large country house, Hatherop Castle, Gloucestershire, into a squash court – Nicholson, of course, was a good squash player himself. The design was plain, and carefully detailed, competent but not challenging. But with his interiors for the Blennerhassetts' house in Elm Park Road, Chelsea, Nicholson seemed almost intoxicated with the fashionable taste of the day (plates 7-9), exploiting many of the stylish new materials – Vitrolite, Bakelite, tinted glass, stainless steel, asbestos – and thus stepping into the shoes of the architect-decorator. EQ helped to choose colours and fabrics, and there must have been a similar close collaboration between them on the studio-flat Nicholson designed for the photographer John Somerset Murray. A photograph by Murray of Christopher in the studio shows patterned cushions and a vividly stripped material covering the curved banquette.

Suddenly this decorative elegance disappeared from his work. Nicholson had arrived at a full commitment to functionalism, joining the small band of Modernists who were starting to make their mark in England. In late 1933, when Nicholson began to design a studio for Augustus John (plates 10-12), his first essay in minimalism, several of his contemporaries had already completed buildings of ruthless rationalism. Nicholson's studio building was indeed a new development, a design capturing the beautiful plastic qualities of Modernism, a small building with a purity of form, line, surface, space and colour, controlled by geometry.

It is no coincidence that at the very moment Nicholson was designing John's studio, his brother Ben was exploring the same aesthetic. As Frances Spalding has commented, Ben Nicholson's carved reliefs and plaster sculptures which he painted white and were composed of layered and juxtaposing circles, squares and rectangles, 'are often regarded as the high point within the history of early modernism in England. Shorn of all extraneous matter, they have a purity sustained by idealism.'[12]

The three-dimensional aspect of Ben Nicholson's work is widely acknowledged to be a result of his new relationship with the sculptor Barbara Hepworth, but his brother's architecture must certainly have been another influence. The cross-currents between the Nicholson brothers are evident in Christopher's drawings for the studio building. Because of its simple requirement for one large space, the scheme is uncomplicated: a room, raised in the Corbusian manner on piloti, and partially encompassed by a terrace. Nicholson's drawings for the plan resemble his brother's reliefs: the studio and terrace are rectangular, broken by a curve – the large window – with a spiral staircase, a three-quarter circle, biting the corner. When Nicholson drew the building in axonometric – a masterly new development for him which now entered his drawing repertoire – the effect was like a Constructivist abstract in three dimensions.

Having broken free from the restraints of traditional drawing methods and presentation while working on John's studio, he was to employ over the next few years a greater variety of materials and mediums, as well as picking up the latest architectural drawing techniques. He began to have his drawings reproduced as blue-prints, a mechanical method which has the effect of looking like a photographic negative, the background rendered dark and his sparse lines in white. Occasionally, he made prints of his designs from linocuts, a medium in which other members of his family were already making names for themselves. Ben Nicholson had created a significant number of lino-block prints, some of which he passed on to their sister Nancy to be printed on fabric. And EQ, too, was a noted fabric designer of lino-block textiles.

Like Ben, Christopher worked on board, and the painterly axonometric drawing of Augustus John's studio reproduced in JM Richards's article on the building in *The Architectural Review*, is one such work.[13] With his design for the Pantheon a few years later, Nicholson created a model of the scheme, had it photographed, mounted on hardboard, and then invited John Piper to paint it (plate 44). Office drawings were regularised, to impart a mechanised aesthetic to their already sparse appearance. Following the new practice introduced by Le Corbusier, stencilling was used extensively. The scheme number was boldly marked, and titles, labelling, measurements, compass points and arrows were inked in with the use of stencils. Sometimes a drawing was rolled into a typewriter for creating blocks of text. And, in the lower right corner *Christopher Nicholson M.A. / Registered Architect / 100 Fulham Road London S.W.3.* was imprinted with a rubber stamp.

Augustus John's studio was important in Nicholson's

development because it gave him his first opportunity to put his theory of geometric proportion into practice. JM Richards, who met up with his school acquaintance when he came to write about John's studio for *The Architectural Review*, spent the first section of his article analysing the architect's system of proportion, 'the familiar one formed by a square and its diagonal'.[14] Modern architects had taken standardisation to heart. For Nicholson it was linked to his belief in the machine as a source of enjoyment, excitement and aesthetic pleasure. Factory-made components, like metal windows, doors and fitments, were becoming part of a systematised way of building. Proportioning had a mystical association, with historical precedence bestowing truth and authenticity. Nicholson's hero Lutyens had developed his own system of proportion which his assistants applied to the sketch designs he handed them to work up into the finished drawing. 'Kit was very sort of geometrical in his design,' recalls Sir Hugh Casson, 'he'd got it from Lutyens really.'[15]

Conformity to a grid system also affected the designs of Nicholson's other two houses, both begun in 1935. Dalingridge Farm, a small country house in Sussex for Miss Katia Freshfield, a childhood acquaintance of EQ's, is one of Nicholson's lesser-known works (plates 29-30). It was given little publicity,[16] no doubt due to its pitched roof – a request of the client – which did not fit the flat-roofed aesthetic of the modern journals. Yet Nicholson lavished all his usual care upon it, neatly creating pure external surfaces employing new materials, standard components and built-in units with hidden hinges and disguised joints.

But it was Kit's Close, the substantial house built for Dr Warren Crowe on the Downs above Henley-on-Thames, Oxfordshire (plates 23-27) which earned Nicholson greater publicity for his experimental views. Photographed, like all his major buildings, by the image-makers of the English moderns, Dell & Wainwright, Kit's

Close received extensive coverage in *The Architectural Review* a year after its completion in 1937.[17] Many of the design drawings, and those done for the *Review*, were covered in the small checkerboard rectangles of patio and roof paving slabs, windows, doors, and cupboards that all conformed to Nicholson's module. When the plans were published in 1937 in *Circle: International Survey of Constructive Art*, the whole surface of the page, except for an insert photograph of the house in construction, was marked off as if it had been drawn on oversized graph paper. There was no commentary; the only words typed onto the drawing indicated the parts of the building and the geometric module: *Scale 12 ' 6 " squares*.[18] The rigorous abstraction of the image was considered just as important as the architecture for the group of artists and architects who published it.

Thus buildings could become giant abstract canvases. Early in his career, Christopher's brother Ben had discovered the potential of colour in Picasso's Cubist paintings and although he eliminated it for a short time in his early abstract reliefs, he soon reintroduced it. The architect Leslie Martin believes that he did so in order that the flat shapes might be given a sense of space.[19] Christopher, however, had no need to express space, architecture being three-dimensional. But colour he could use, hence the brick walls of Augustus John's studio were painted pink, with only the thin lines of the concrete frame in white. Kit's Close was an altogether more ambitious abstract work. In plan, the house is a series of interlocking rectangles which effectively produce large blank walls protruding from the major elevations. At certain points these solid masses are pierced by small circles, the porthole windows. The walls, of rendered plaster, were then painted a warm brick colour, the coping in plum red, and the windows on the other walls an off-white. When Nicholson completed the London Gliding Club, he chose to paint it green. These buildings when freshly executed were like colourful abstract paintings in the landscape.

Nicholson was somewhat reticent about proselytising his architectural sentiments, and only published one article on airport design after the War.[20] He restricted his architectural membership to the professional body of the Royal Institute of British Architects, and the Modern Architectural Research (MARS) group, and just before he died he joined the Society of Industrial Artists. Although Nicholson's work was published in *Circle*, a book edited by Ben Nicholson, Leslie Martin and the sculptor Naum Gabo, Christopher was not specifically part of the Circle group.[21] He was, however, very sympathetic to the group's desire to create a closer alliance between art, science and architecture.

Most of the architects loosely associated with the Circle were members of the MARS group which was formed in 1933. Nicholson did not seek election until 1937, and this was probably more from his wish to take part in the group's 1938 exhibition[22] (plate 41) than from any real desire to create rousing manifestos. Moreover, many of his architectural friends were part of MARS – Leslie Martin, Misha Black, Wells Coates and Basil Spence, as well as critics and historians like Herbert Read and John Summerson, who was to become Ben Nicholson's sister-in-law's husband at the end of 1938. Christopher was naturally included in such important events as the farewell dinner given in March 1937 to Walter Gropius on the eve of his departure to America.

Nicholson delivered his most public exposition of his architectural ideology when he taught the course 'Orientation Towards Modern Architecture' at the Ozenfant Academy sometime during 1936 or 1937. The Purist painter Amédée Ozenfant was yet another refugee from the political upheavals on the Continent, and like Gropius, Mendelsohn and Breuer, stayed in England for a few years before emigrating to the United States. Ozenfant, who had collaborated with Le Corbusier in co-editing *L'Esprit Nouveau*, was a leading theorist on the psychological methods of perceiving colour and form. At his new Academy in London, which he opened after the closure of his Paris Académie, he favoured the integration of the arts. Nicholson's role was to introduce artists, sculptors, decorators, typographers, draughtsmen, and those working in publicity, to the connection between architecture and their particular field. He spoke about the traditions and 'necessity' of modern architecture, building methods both ancient and modern, the 'mechanics' of modern building, modern economic and social requirements, and the responsibility of the architect.[23]

Nicholson had himself expanded into a related field where many architects feel naturally at home – furniture design. Furniture is sculpture, it is about structure and materials, and like building, it is a practical art. Nicholson's built-in pieces, which were mainly cupboards, followed the standard modern format of being as discreet as possible. His first free-standing desks and cabinets, however, were monumental in form, and of an architectural nature. His design for a radiogram (plate 14) of about 1934, is composed of interlocking blocks and is thus comparable, for example, to Kit's Close. As he learned more about modern furniture-making techniques, especially how to bend and mould plywood, Nicholson developed light-weight pieces along the lines of Breuer, Mathsson and Aalto. During 1934 and 1935, he designed a table and chair for the Pioneer Health Centre (plates 18-20), which were made economically using plywood cut-outs. It was not until he began to design for Heal's and Isokon, both furniture companies with their own modern lines, that Nicholson applied the new technology to his chair designs (plates 15-16, 42).

The radios and television sets which Nicholson designed after the Second World War for Ferranti were treated like pieces of furniture (plates 76-80). His advanced design aesthetic and fascination with new materials suited a company working at the cutting edge of technology. He was also familiar with electronic equipment.

During the War, Nicholson piloted almost every type of British aeroplane made at the time and was attracted by the dazzling display of indicators, gauges and switches to be found in their cockpits. For each radio, television and radiogram, Nicholson made dozens of alternative designs, playing with the simple shapes of rectangular dial and grille, the round knobs and the square picture screen. Ben's abstracts had been translated into product design.

Flying, especially gliding, was as important as architecture in Nicholson's life. He had taken up flying at Cambridge and gliding in 1931. The merger of his two greatest interests resulted in one of his most famous works, the London Gliding Club, sited at the foot of the Dunstable Downs in Bedfordshire (plates 33-39). The challenge was to design, on a tight budget, a substantial building providing hangar space for up to thirty sailplanes together with club accommodation. Nicholson's solution is as beautiful as it is practical, being dependent upon the simplicity of integrating standard-sized factory components – windows, doors, wall sheeting and light fittings – into a compact plan. JM Richards, in his extensive review of the London Gliding Club, expressed a fascination with the manner in which Nicholson stated the construction through internal finishes. For example, in the lounge, the girder which spanned the hangar below formed the sill of the ribbon windows which, in turn, were finished with a strip of linoleum glued immediately on top, 'the effect of which, as of the rest of the room is one of neatness and serviceableness without ever degenerating into crudity.'[24] Richards also introduced his article with a section entitled 'Gliding: A Social Activity: The Programme and its Solution', in which he compared gliding and architecture as a case of 'different forms of similar scientific adventure, that offers a rare opportunity for homogeneity between form and function.' Art and technology meet once again.

Hugh Casson joined his former Cambridge tutor to

assist on the gliding club, and was responsible for the more routine work like kitchens and lavatories. Casson recalls how if Nicholson was tremendously interested in some aspect of the design, like creating a solution to how to place the lounge over the hangar,

> he might get crazy with interest and then he held it to his bosom and he'd do it himself. He liked doing it right down to the skirting boards ... He was always more experienced than I was ... and being that sort of mechanically-minded chap he might be doing working drawings of door handles, which I was rather bad at.[25]

The excitement of Nicholson's design for the gliding club inspired Casson to create some of his finest architectural drawings.

Casson's presence in the office seemed to double the pleasure Nicholson took in life. 'I was devoted to him', says Casson, 'because he was wonderfully giggly, and it was really a hilarious time.'[26] Casson also brought a different sensibility to Nicholson's office drawings, a light-hearted but never frivolous approach which began to emerge when they received the commission to alter Monkton House for Edward James (plates 21-22). James and Salvador Dali, the Surrealist painter who also contributed to the design, used to visit Nicholson and Casson in the office to discuss, and joke about, the project. The quirky nature of the scheme appealed to Casson's humour – rooms with breathing walls, exploding swans on the lake – and he seems to have taken on much of the job. A few years later, James again turned to Nicholson for another scheme, re-erecting Wyatt's dismantled eighteenth century facade of the Pantheon with a modern house behind, which sadly was not carried out. Nicholson's proportional approach to architecture was at odds with Monkton's picturesque fantasy and better suited to the Pantheon's classicism, making it easier for him to design a rational modern building behind a rational classical front.

The case of Monkton and the Pantheon highlight the interesting differences between Nicholson and Casson: one was an architect dedicated to proportion and abstraction, while the other was more interested in informality and the representational. But the two temperaments were complementary. Tension rarely shows in the projects they worked on together because Nicholson retained full control over the finished design. It is mainly in the drawings that any dichotomy is evident. Casson's perspectives are drawn with agile brushwork, illustrative skill and bright colours, thus transforming Nicholson's disciplined designs into lyrical performances. Nicholson was in tune with the abstract painters, Casson with the New Romantics like John Piper and Graham Sutherland.

With the outbreak of war in September 1939, Nicholson closed the office and joined the Royal Naval Volunteer Reserve where he was commissioned a Lieutenant in the Fleet Air Arm. Service discipline suited him and he was able to indulge his passion for flying. At first he trained as a meteorological officer (plate 50) and was then assigned as a flight deck officer on board HMS *Kenya*. In June 1941 he was discharged from ship duties and appointed to 756 Squadron with whom he flew for the next four years based at Royal Naval Air Stations at Lee-on-Solent and Worthy Down in southern England, then as Lieutenant Commander at Crail in Scotland, Commander of Inskip, Lancashire, and finally, in January 1945, in charge of the station at Katukurunda, Ceylon. His pilot's log book is a roll-call of the aircraft he flew: Spitfire, Tiger Moth, Vega, Hurricane, Proctor, Beaufighter, Blenheim, Oxford, Firefly, Gladiator, Beaufort, Hellcat, Reliant, Wellington. These machines were like flying works of architecture for Nicholson.

During the War, Nicholson had little opportunity to design, although from on board HMS *Kenya* he proudly wrote to Ben in St Ives that the ship was full of 'the latest gadgets and is still the most modern of her kind in the fleet . . . and now has a sick-bay modified to my design (which looks like being adopted in her many sister-ships).'[27] He flew solo in a Hellcat from England to his assignment in Ceylon, a month's travel by way of Libya, Egypt, the Persian Gulf and straight down the middle of India. On the journey he stopped at the Castel Benito in Tripoli where he saw the Fascist military architecture. He observed that it was 'mostly simple in design but so coarsely dimensioned that the scale is ruined and a vacuous feeling produced.' Again, proportion was the most important factor when he had an exciting experience sleeping in a Middle Eastern hut of local native construction.

> One day I'm going to imitate it. Reinforced in bamboo and, though of course very small, dimensioned in the grand manner. Scale absolutely no objection. I've made a drawing of it and one day you'll be surprised![28]

When he was discharged from the services in September 1945, Nicholson's long-standing friendship with Whitney Straight earned him a position as consultant to the newly created British European Airways. Straight was the deputy chairman, and Nicholson's fellow glider pilot from Dunstable, Philip Wills, was technical manager and head of research. Nicholson, rejoined by Casson, found an office at 110 Old Brompton Road early in 1946, and for BEA they set about designing ticket offices in Paris, Stockholm and Glasgow (plates 53-55), interior finishes and exterior livery for the fleet (plates 56-59), and an assortment of miscellaneous design assignments which went along with producing a corporate image (plates 60-65). With his concurrent engagement for Ferranti,

Christopher Nicholson had moved successfully into the field of industrial design.

The bread and butter of Nicholson's existence before the war had been the dozens of small alterations and additions he made to flats and houses for his extensive network of family and friends. From 1946 to his death in 1948, the little job earners were exhibition stands (plates 67-71). With Britain gearing up for a post-war boom, which took a very long while to materialise, the industrial propaganda of exhibitions served to promote optimism in the face of austerity.

Nicholson and Casson now took on assistants, including Neville Conder and Gontran Goulden. Sometimes these young architects brought in their own jobs, or at busy moments lent a hand on such projects as the Experimental Laboratory at Wexham Springs, Buckinghamshire, which Nicholson had on the drawing table when he died (plate 75).

After the war, Nicholson took on more duties within the profession. For the RIBA he served as an external examiner and member of the Board of Architectural Education. He taught for the winter term of 1945 and spring term of 1946 at the Architectural Association. It was on behalf of the AA, in February 1946, that he travelled to Paris where he visited Le Corbusier's office, paid homage to Auguste Perret, and 'saw André Lurçat and thought his re-planning schemes very bad and he himself very superficial about contemporary architecture.'[29]

In May 1948, Nicholson was elected to the AA Council. On 11 June 1948, he wrote to his brother Ben that he was off to Switzerland for the gliding championship. 'Wish me luck,' he said.[30]

1 Quoted in John Rothenstein, *Modern English Painters*, I, 1952, p41.

2 Tate Gallery Archive. Ben Nicholson papers. 8717.1.1.520. Letter, not dated; see also Philip Wills, *On Being a Bird*, 1953, p169 and Ann Welch, *The Story of Gliding*, 1980 (2nd ed.), pp161-64.

3 Private collection. Letter from Casson to Nicholson, 13 July 1948.

4 York City Art Gallery, *The Nicholsons: A Story of Four People and their Designs*, 1988, p15.

5 Both the Mabel Pryde and William Orpen paintings are in the National Galleries of Scotland.

6 JM Richards, *Memoirs of an Unjust Fellow*, 1980, pp34-35.

7 Jeremy Lewison, *Ben Nicholson*, Tate Gallery catalogue, 1993, p242. It was designed to be played on a small table in a constricted space.

8 Ibid. pp239-40.

9 Tate Gallery Archive. Ben Nicholson papers. 8717.1.1.933. Letter, 18 May 1930.

10 Notes made by the author of a conversation with Sir Thomas Bazley, 19 June 1995.

11 Letter to the author from Mrs Deenagh Goold-Adams (née Blennerhassett), 31 January 1995.

12 F Spalding, *British Art Since 1900*, 1986, p110.

13 *The Architectural Review*, LXXVII, 1935, pp65-68.

14 Ibid. p65.

15 Recorded conversation by Cathy Courtney with Sir Hugh Casson, 13 February 1986, for the National Life Story Collection, British Library National Sound Archive. Transcript C408/016/F1087-A, p82.

16 *Architect & Building News*, CLV, 1938, pp42-43.

17 *The Architectural Review*, LXXXIII, 1938, pp305-09.

18 J Leslie Martin, Ben Nicholson and Naum Gabo, editors, *Circle: International Survey of Constructive Art*, 1937, p38.

19 Lewison, *op cit*, p221.

20 Christopher Nicholson and Major R Mealing, *Architect & Building News*, CLVIII, 1939, pp377-80 and CLIX, pp16-20 (including Nicholson's design for an airport) and 49-51. Hugh Casson recalls the effort of writing it 'absolutely killed him.' (Quoted in Tim Nicholson, 'Christopher Nicholson: Pre-War Work', sixth year dissertation, School of Architecture, Thames Polytechnic, 1978, p79.)

21 Notes made by the author of a conversation with Sir Leslie Martin, 26 January 1996.

22 See *The Architectural Review*, LXXXIII, 1938, p116.

23 Printed prospectus on the Ozenfant Academy in RIBA Manuscripts & Archives Collection, Ernö Goldfinger papers, box 23, folder 3.

24 *The Architectural Review*, LXXIX, 1936, pp254-62.

25 Recorded conversation by the author with Sir Hugh Casson, 12 January 1995.

26 Recorded conversation by Cathy Courtney with Sir Hugh Casson, *op cit*.

27 Tate Gallery Archive. Ben Nicholson papers. 8717.1.1.942. Letter, 15 January 1940 [should be 1941].

28 Private collection: Mss typescript of letter begun 27 February 1945.

29 Tate Gallery Archive. Ben Nicholson papers. 8717.1.1.950. Letter to Ben Nicholson, 24 February 1946.

30 Ibid. 8717.1.1.955.

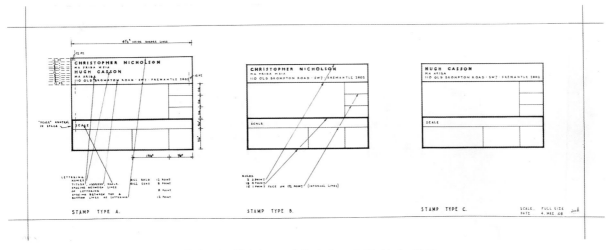

Christopher Nicholson and Hugh Casson's title blocks, 1948

PLATES

1. Student design for a municipal observatory, 1926-27

This drawing survives only as a photographic glass negative

Having completed three years at the Cambridge School of Architecture, Nicholson gained a scholarship to study for a year at Princeton. This student design project for an observatory shows how successfully he absorbed American sources, most particularly in the planning which is overwhelmingly Beaux Arts influenced, the dominant style then being taught in the American schools of architecture. The principal building is a clash of French revolutionary architecture and the jazzy new Art Deco, straight from the Paris International Exhibition of 1925. But the greatest Americanism is the dedication carved beneath the upper terrace which proclaims that the observatory is to be erected to the genius of Mr Newton – poor Sir Isaac has been democratised.

2. Design for the garden house for Charles Roberts, Boothby, Brampton, Cumbria, 1928

Pencil, brown wash and red crayon (395 × 445)

Like many young architects, Nicholson gained his first jobs through family connections. His brother Ben's first wife, the painter Winifred Roberts, was a cousin of the 10th Earl of Carlisle, and had a cottage near her parents' house, Boothby, which in turn was on the estate of Naworth Castle, the Carlisle seat. Christopher stayed often with Ben and Winifred during the late 1920s, sketching and making measured drawings of the local buildings, which explains the vernacular treatment of this garden house. With its rubblestone walls and steeply pitched roof, the design is also reminiscent of Lutyens's garden houses at Abbotswood and The Hoo. Nicholson's love of Lutyens's architecture always remained, even after he had turned to Continental Modernism.

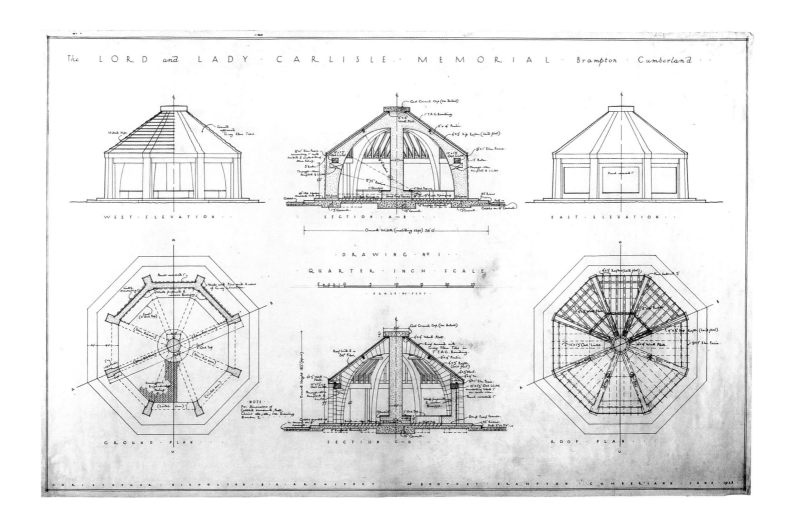

3. Design for the Carlisle Memorial, Brampton, Cumbria, 1928

Pen on linen (550 × 875)

This was Nicholson's first major commission, and his diary for the period is filled with worried entries about details and construction. The memorial to the 9th Earl and Countess of Carlisle is a wayside shelter for travellers, and stands at a crossroads near the town of Brampton, close to the Carlisle seat of Naworth Castle. The octagonal shaped structure is like a tent with buttressing. Walls, piers and arches are of grey limestone and pivot around a central stone column which is capped by a cast concrete slab. The rafters and seating are in oak.

4. Design for a library fireplace, Hatherop Castle, Gloucestershire, for Sir Thomas Bazley, 1932

Pencil and brown wash, mounted (160 × 160)

Nicholson struck up a great friendship with Sir Thomas, who had inherited Hatherop Castle, a massive forty-four bedroom pile which had been rebuilt following a fire in the mid-nineteenth century by the architect Henry Clutton. Sir Thomas Bazley only required a few fireplaces at first, but went on to commission the conversion of a conservatory into a squash court where he and Nicholson played furious sets. After the War, Sir Thomas also asked Nicholson to design a village centre (plate 66).

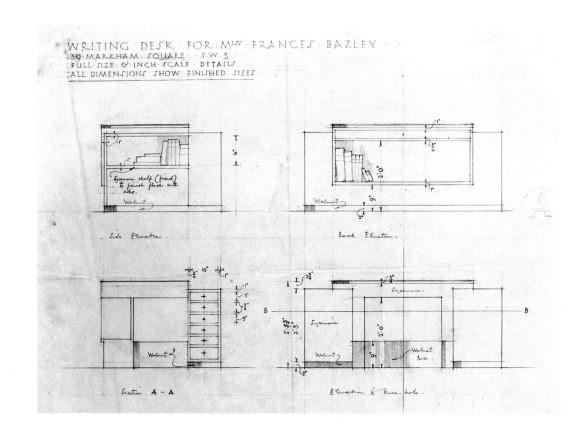

5. Design for a writing desk for Miss Frances Bazley, c1931

Pencil, pen and red crayon on tracing paper (485 × 435), detail

This writing desk has no legs and stands like a monumental work of architecture, solid and flat upon the ground. The 'elevation to knee-hole' (lower right) could be the facade design for a large civic building or public institution in the favoured stripped classicism of the 1920s and early thirties. There is nothing feminine about Miss Bazley's desk, built of sycamore and walnut with a thick plate glass top and deep shelving back and sides to take heavy tomes. It must have been the devil to move when she got married in 1932.

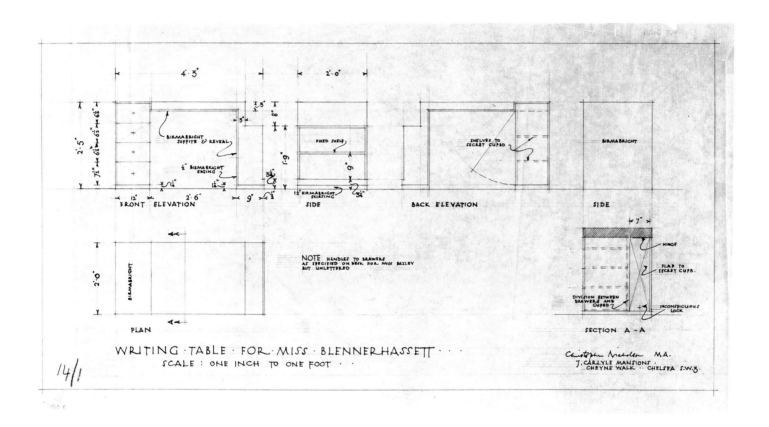

WRITING · TABLE · FOR · MISS · BLENNERHASSETT · · ·
SCALE : ONE INCH TO ONE FOOT · ·

6. Design for a writing table for Deenagh Blennerhassett, *c* 1933

Pen, pencil and red crayon on tracing paper (275 × 525)

Nicholson designed this extremely fashionable writing table for his wife's cousin, the sixteen year old Miss Blennerhassett. Much of the table was covered in Birma Bright, a new light aluminium-based alloy produced by Messrs Gibbins Ltd of Wolverhampton. Invented in the 1920s for use in non-corrosive situations, Birma Bright was just beginning to attract Modern architects who appreciated its machine aesthetic. Its surface was polished a grey-white colour. The rest of the table was painted pale lemon yellow. Miss Blennerhassett recalls that the secret cupboard, accessible by swinging back the reveal flap, was intended, hopefully, for love letters.

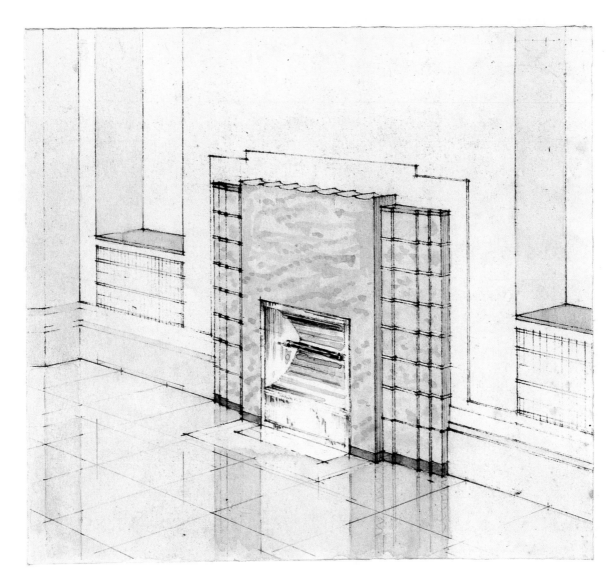

7. Preliminary design for the sitting room fireplace and radiator casings, 74 Elm Park Road, London, for Richard Blennerhassett, 1933

Print with pencil and coloured washes added (170 × 185)

Having recently moved into a large Victorian house in Chelsea, the client asked Nicholson to modernise it. Making few structural alterations, Nicholson concentrated on giving Mrs Blennerhassett a fashionable bedroom suite and installing central heating. The unsightly hot water radiators were generally enclosed within flat modern surfaces like built-in window seats or, as here, by a detachable Birma

Bright frame with a wire mesh front, topped with a travertine shelf. Many of the obsolete fireplaces were redesigned. In this instance, the surround is made of painted, laminated board with horizontal stainless steel trim decorating the sides. And, appropriate to Mr Blennerhassett's position as an engineer with the Edmundson Electricity Corporation, a shiny new electric fire was installed.

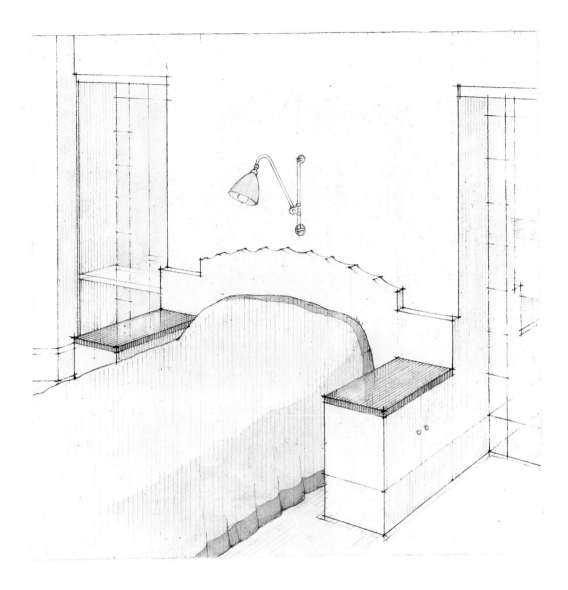

8. Design for bed-head and mirrored recesses for Mrs Blennerhassett's bedroom, 74 Elm Park Road, London, 1933

Print with pencil and coloured washes added (235 × 235)

The geometry of Nicholson's design for Mrs Blennerhassett's bedroom is broken only by the sleepy ripple of the bed-head. This *plus moderne* interior, influenced no doubt by the architect's many visits to Paris, has been arranged to take advantage of the removal of the fireplace. The bed-head is built over the old opening and the recesses on either side of the chimney breast used as built-in boudoir furniture: on one side, as a dressing table, and on the other,

for a wash basin, discreetly not shown in this perspective. Mirrors backed the recesses, stainless steel edged the angles, the reveals were lined with Vitrolite and the table top with black Bakelite. The effect was sparkling. Lighting was concealed with the exception of the adjustable Bestlite by Best and Lloyd. Nicholson's wife, the designer and painter EQ, found the furnishing fabrics for Mrs and Miss Blennerhassett from which to make a choice.

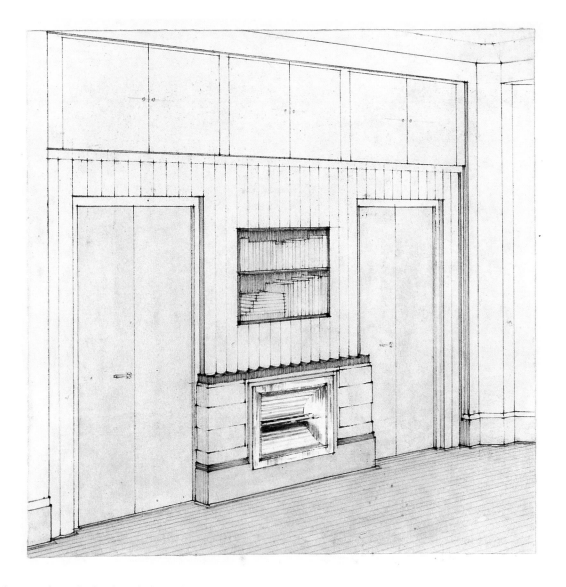

9. Preliminary design for fitted wardrobes and electric fire surround for Mrs Blennerhassett's bedroom, 74 Elm Park Road, London 1933

Print with pencil and coloured washes added (235 × 235)

The Blennerhassetts sold much of their old-fashioned furniture when they moved into their new house in Chelsea. Out went the free-standing wardrobes, replaced by Nicholson's built-in units. One set of doors opened onto a space for hanging clothes, the other to racks of sliding trays. In the executed version of this design, the wall fluting was dispensed with and the electric fire surround given a sparkling stainless steel reveal and hearth. The whole was set off by a decorated asbestos surround.

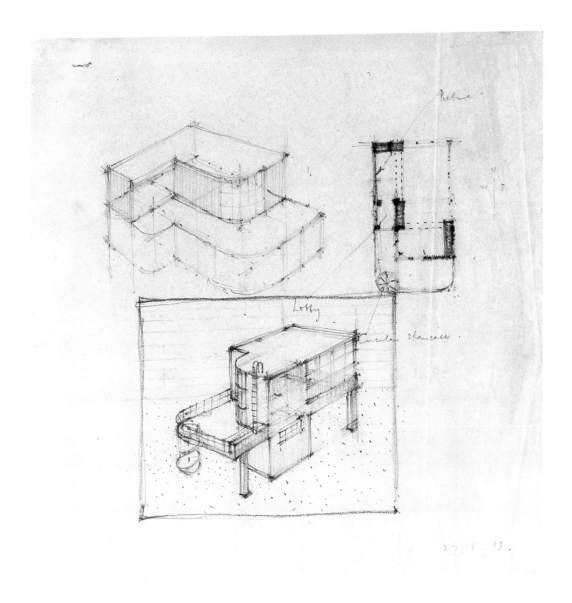

10. Preliminary design for the studio, Fryern Court, Fordingbridge, Hampshire, for Augustus John, 1933

Pencil and red crayon on a sketchbook page (260 × 250)

Christopher's father, the painter William Nicholson, and Augustus John were friends. Hence this commission for a studio building in the garden of John's house outside Fordingbridge. Nicholson was familiar with the studio world, knowledgable in its subtle requirements for space and light. In this early sketch, the basic plan of a large open room with a curving corner window has emerged. The style is uncompromisingly modern, and follows the Corbusian dictate of raising the structure on piloti to give a clear space beneath, which was more than an aesthetic decision in this case as the building was among trees and needed to be raised into the light.

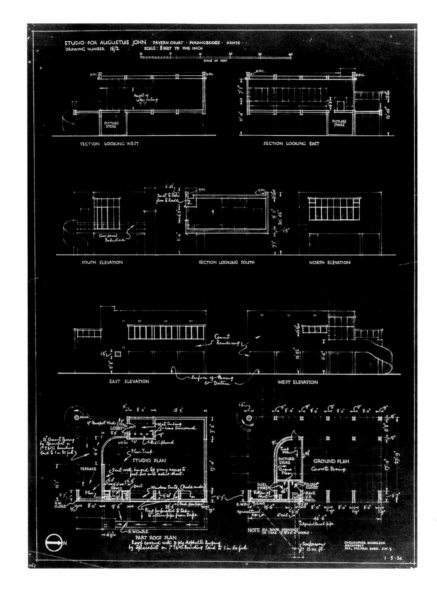

11. Design for the studio, Fryern Court, Fordingbridge, Hampshire, for Augustus John, 1934
Blueprint (560 × 420)

The two plans at the bottom of this blueprint are scored with the grid pattern of the paving slabs – each measuring 2 foot by 2 foot 10 inches. This was the measurement of the proportional system which embraces Nicholson's whole design for Augustus John's studio. The rational methodology gives the building an architectural coherence, although it was Nicholson's expressive sense of design which gave it a soul. Structurally, the studio is held within a reinforced concrete frame, with walls infilled with brick. Nicholson defined the construction materials by colour: the concrete skeleton was painted white and the brickwork in a light pink. The only feature breaking into the large interior space of the studio room was a pair of piers between the east windows, supporting the large service duct overhead and reflecting the light around the artist's workspace.

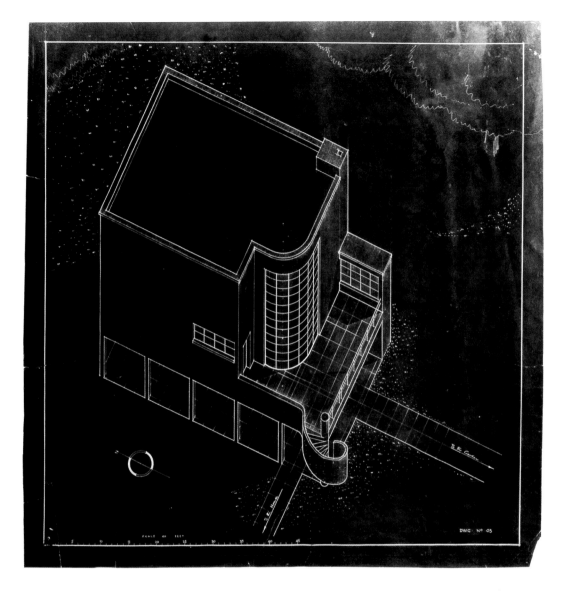

12. Design for the studio, Fryern Court, Fordingbridge, Hampshire, for Augustus John, *c*1934

Blueprint (600 × 590)

The thin line of this spare axonometric blueprint closely evokes the simplicity of the building's design. Christopher Nicholson's image bears an artistic similarity to the abstract drawings of the same period by his brother Ben. Both Nicholsons were absorbed in the play of geometric harmony as derived from angles and curves, and in this design for Augustus John's studio the curvature of spiral staircase and corner window break the deliberate grid-plan of the architect's repeating rectangle.

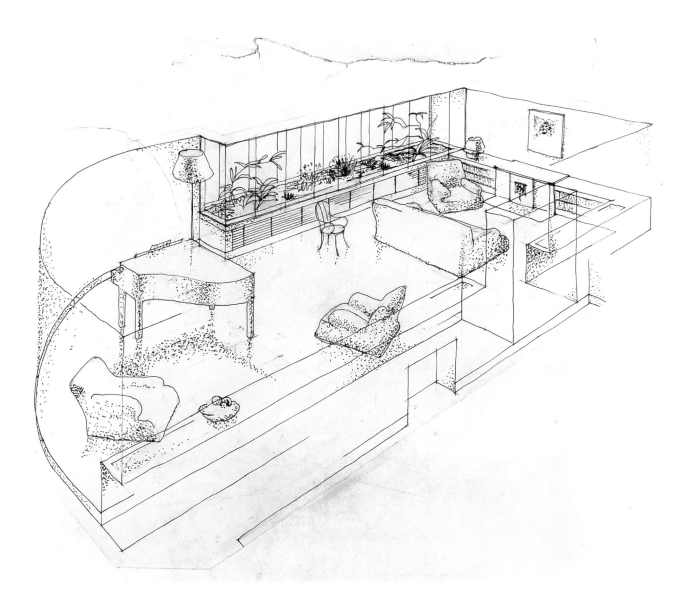

13. Preliminary design for a library, Fryern Court, Fordingbridge, Hampshire, for Augustus John, 1935

Pen, pencil, red pencil and stencil (360 × 530, mounted)

Pleased with the studio which Nicholson had built for him, Augustus John asked the architect back to Fryern Court to design a library. This early drawing for the scheme shows the room as seen through the transparent walls of the existing house. With its curving wall, echoed in the shape of the grand piano, the library plan is reminiscent of the studio building in the garden. In its final form, the plant-filled conservatory in front of the window was replaced by a more practical seat.

14. Design for a radiogram unit, *c* 1934

Pen and wash, pencil and black crayon on a sketchbook page (275 × 290), detail

This design appears to be for a custom-designed unit, as opposed to a prototype for manufacture. It would have housed a radio, and perhaps a gramophone, with integral bookshelves. Behind the closed doors may well have been a cocktail cabinet. The client could have been the Blennerhassets for whom Nicholson was doing similar pieces of furniture. During the 1930s, many architects designed such massive units in order to integrate and match the latest technological equipment within an advanced room setting.

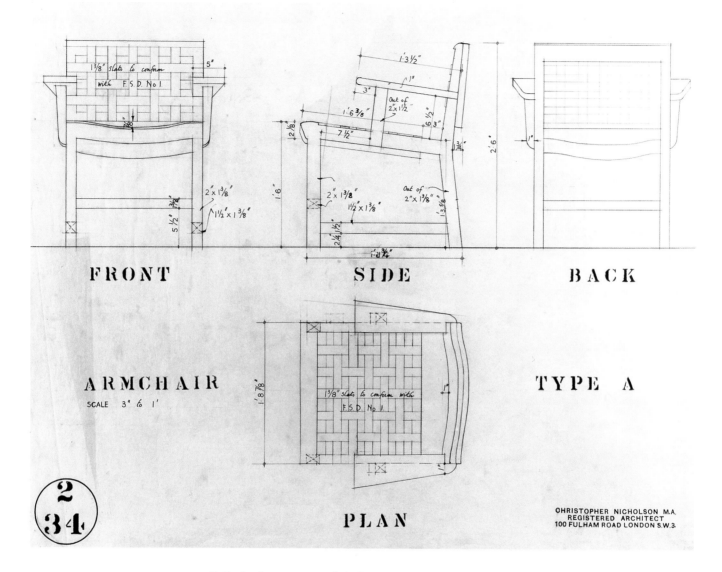

FRONT   SIDE   BACK

ARMCHAIR   TYPE A

SCALE 3" to 1'

PLAN

CHRISTOPHER NICHOLSON M.A.
REGISTERED ARCHITECT
100 FULHAM ROAD LONDON S.W.3.

15. Design for terrace armchair, for Messrs Heal and Son Ltd, 1935

Pencil, red pen, green stencil and office stamp on detail paper (510 × 650)

This terrace armchair was made and sold by Heal's. It was part of a set of four pieces that Nicholson created for Sir Ambrose Heal which featured in the exhibition 'Contemporary Furniture Designed by 7 Architects' in 1936, organised by Maxwell Fry and including room settings by Marcel Breuer, Raymond McGrath and Brian O'Rorke. The armchair is a hybrid work, combining a traditional thick teak frame with woven, modern-inspired slatting. Nicholson's terrace seating was sold by Heal's until the War.

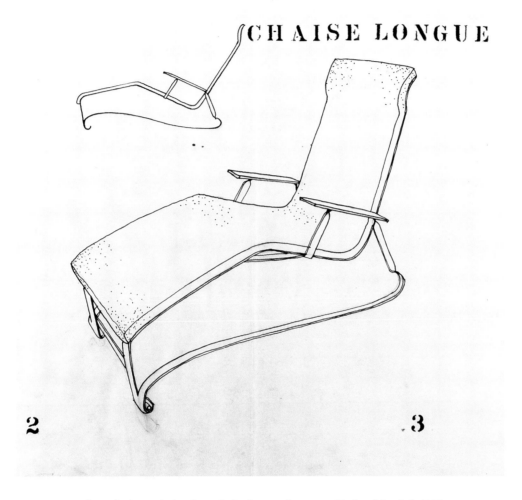

CHAISE LONGUE

2   3

16. Preliminary design for a chaise longue, for Messrs Heal and Son Ltd, 1935

Pen, pencil (rubbed out) and stencil on detail paper (535 × 1600), detail

Nicholson was smack up-to-date and highly innovative in his design for this aluminium framed chaise longue. The earlier phase of modern furniture design had favoured tubular steel, but by the early 1930s, aluminium banding was becoming the new experimental material. To form each side of Nicholson's chair, a long aluminium strip has been cut down the centre and then stretched apart, the top half still joined to the bottom runner at the curl of the front foot. The twist of the metal at the rear angle was aesthetic and structural, placed at a point of maximum stress. Although tubular steel was used when manufactured, this chair is one of Nicholson's finest pieces of furniture.

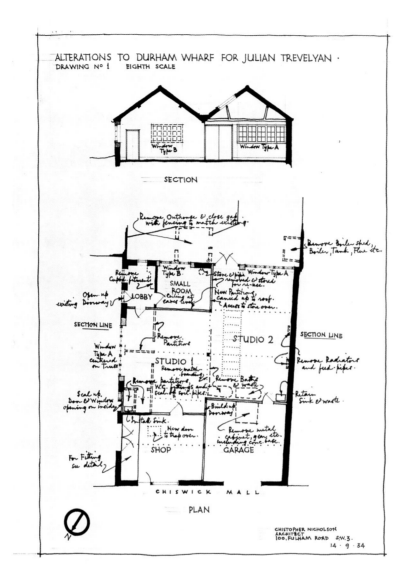

17. Design for alterations to Durham Wharf, Chiswick Mall, London, for Julian Trevelyan, 1934

Pen and wash on tracing paper (425 × 295)

The artist Julian Trevelyan and his wife, the potter Ursula Darwin, were newly married when they found Durham Wharf, a Thames-side boathouse. Trevelyan turned to his friend to convert the boathouse into studios and a shop. For the first few years, the Trevelyans used the studios for their own work and etching classes, and the shop for renting out pictures they bought in Paris, Trevelyan having recently lived there. Nicholson also inserted a large metal-frame window in the house, at the end of the sitting room, to give panoramic views directly onto the river. Today, Julian Trevelyan's second wife, the painter Mary Fedden, lives and works in Durham Wharf.

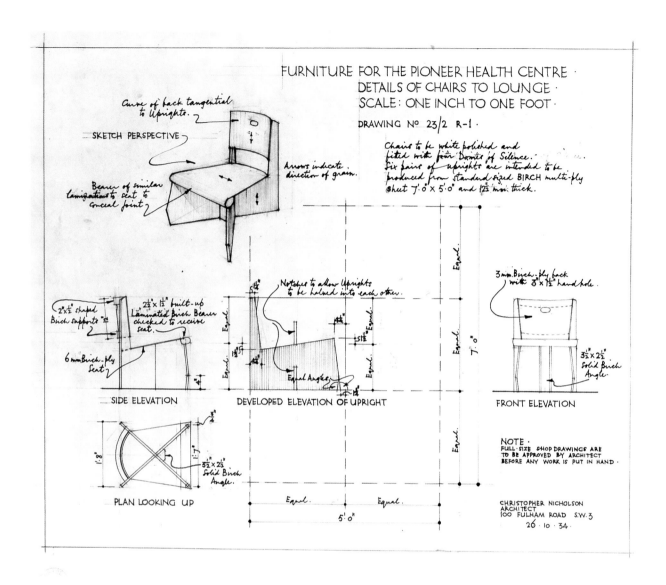

18. Design for a chair, Pioneer Health Centre, Peckham, London, 1934

Pen and pencil on detail paper (385 × 430)

This is Nicholson's economical solution to mass produced chairs for the Pioneer Health Centre. Two flat shaped pieces of birch plywood slot over each other to form the structure. In the centre of this drawing, the 'Developed Elevation of Upright' illustrates how these slotted shapes were cut from a standard size of sheet plywood so that there was no wastage. On to this structure were fitted a flat seat and bentwood back, both upholstered in 'dunlopillo' sponge rubber. The cross shape of the chair is probably a deliberate structural derivation of the supports of the building itself, reinforced concrete columns designed by the engineer Sir Owen Williams in a cruciform shape.

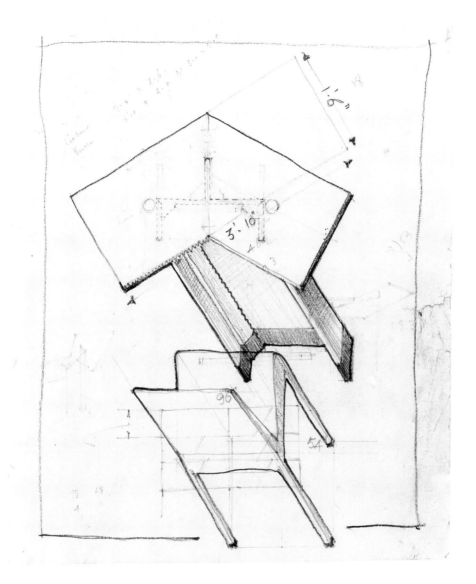

19. Preliminary design for table and chair, Pioneer Health Centre, Peckham, London, 1934-35

Pencil and red crayon on detail paper on a sketchbook page (295 × 250)

This is an early design for the standard table and chair used throughout the Pioneer Health Centre. Like the Centre itself, Nicholson's furniture was a social and economic experiment: a health and recreational enterprise for working class families in south London, based on the benefits of community interaction, with furniture designed for its flexibility of arrangement and made at a moderate cost. The design for the chair in this drawing is fairly conventional, and evolved into a more complex and easy-to-build piece. The table, however, has begun to achieve its final form, but lacks the simple and more stable solution of the final design.

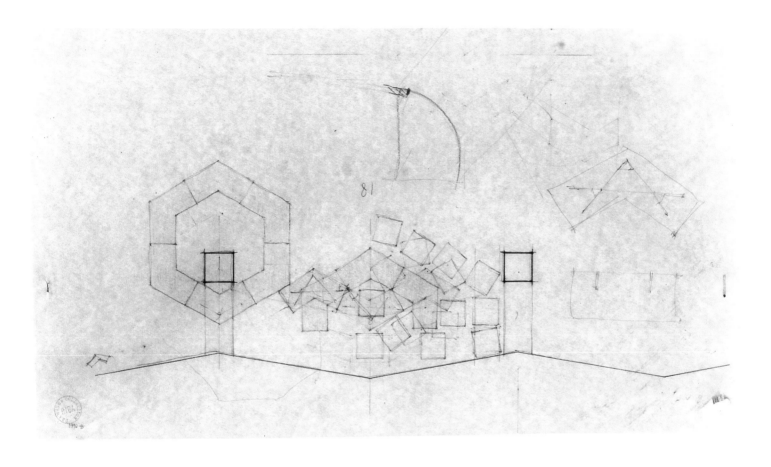

20. Sketch design for suggested arrangements of tables and chairs, Pioneer Health Centre, Peckham, London, 1934-35

Pencil and red, green and blue crayon on tracing paper (380 × 535), detail

Flexibility, open circulation, freedom of plan – these were the characteristics which Sir Owen Williams successfully achieved with his design for the Pioneer Health Centre, and which Nicholson emulated when he created the Centre's furniture. In this drawing the swarming forms are Nicholson's suggestions for how his tables and chairs might cluster and interlock in a variety of patterns. The chairs are the square forms, and the tables the shape of arrowheads. To achieve such an abstract concept, in both this drawing and execution, shows how strongly Nicholson had absorbed his brother Ben's recent developments in complete geometric abstractionism.

21. Design for Monkton House, West Dean, West Sussex, by Edwin Lutyens, 1902, with later additions by Christopher Nicholson, 1935

Print with pencil, pen and coloured washes added (555 × 720), detail

The conversion of Monkton House from a pretty Lutyens country house to a bizarre surrealist retreat must be one of the oddest commissions any architect has received this century. The client was Edward James, a rich and eccentric aesthete who had introduced the fantastic and distorted paintings of Salvador Dali to the London art world. James asked Dali to design alterations to Monkton House, getting Nicholson and Casson to cope with the architectural execution. In this original print from Lutyens's office, the first touches of metamorphosis have begun to appear with the pencilled-in sculpted sheets thrown out of the first floor windows like laundry hung out to dry. Together, the architects, client and surrealist painter added simulated bamboo columns and palm trees to the facade.

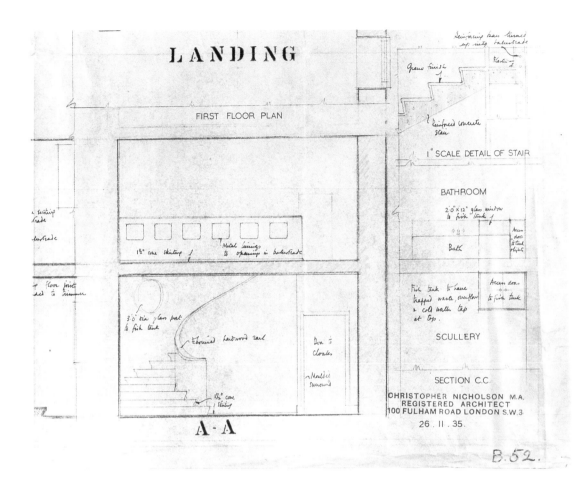

22. Design for alterations and additions to Monkton House, West Dean, West Sussex, for Edward James, 1935
Print with coloured crayon added (680 × 910), detail

These sections are for the amusing new staircase and bathroom in Edward James's surrealist country house. It was Hugh Casson who solved the technical problem posed by the client and Salvador Dali of how to design a 3 foot porthole window looking into an illuminated fish tank half way up the curving flight of stairs. The tank was very deep and extended up into the bathroom, so that whoever was sitting in the bath was pressed up against the large aquarium window with fish swimming by. Equally entertaining was the possibility of catching a glimpse of people bathing as you ascended the staircase.

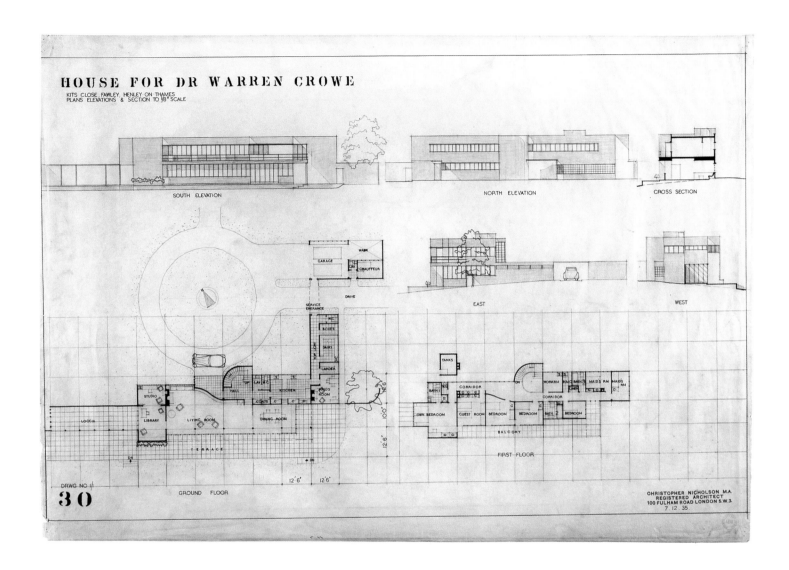

HOUSE FOR DR WARREN CROWE

KITS CLOSE, FAWLEY, HENLEY-ON-THAMES
PLANS ELEVATIONS & SECTION TO 1/8" SCALE

SOUTH ELEVATION

NORTH ELEVATION

CROSS SECTION

EAST

WEST

GROUND FLOOR

FIRST FLOOR

DRWG NO 11
30

CHRISTOPHER NICHOLSON M.A.
REGISTERED ARCHITECT
100 FULHAM ROAD LONDON S.W.3.
7.12.35.

23. Design for Kit's Close, Fawley Green, Oxfordshire, for Dr Warren Crowe, 1935

Pen, pencil, yellow crayon, stencil and office stamp on detail paper (660 × 975)

Kit's Close is one of Britain's major Modern Movement houses of the 1930s. The client was Dr Warren Crowe who, with his wife Virginia, encouraged Nicholson's brand of Modernism in what proved to be the architect's largest private commission. During the winter of 1935-36, Nicholson made a series of designs for the house, of which this one is almost as executed. The basic concept remained constant in all the designs: an L-shaped plan with the larger wing containing the living and dining rooms on the ground floor and principal bedrooms above, and the service wing placed on the angle to the rear. The plans at the bottom of the drawing are overlaid with a pencil grid showing Nicholson's 12 foot 6 inch proportional module, only broken by a 10 foot section through the principal rooms.

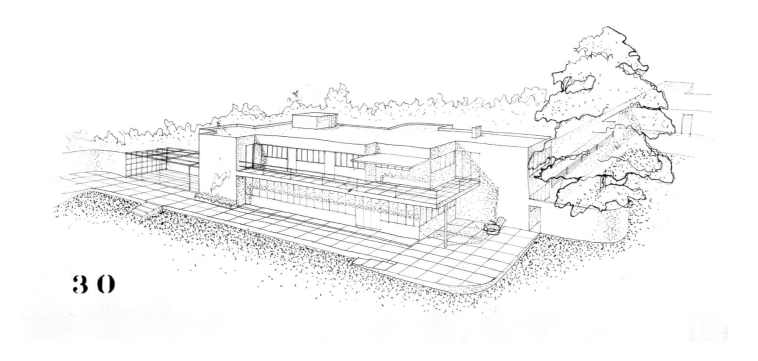

24. Perspective of south front for Kit's Close, Fawley Green, Oxfordshire, 1935

Pen, yellow and blue crayon, stencil and office stamp on detail paper (340 × 760)

Although Christopher Nicholson was called 'Kit' by his family and friends, the name Kit's Close was coincidental, this being the name of the field which Dr Crowe bought on the edge of the village of Fawley Green, near Henley. This drawing, like its companion perspective for the early design in plate 23, is by Hugh Casson. It clearly shows the importance that Nicholson gave to the exterior 'rooms' of the house: the terrace, loggia and balcony which are all picked out in a strong arrangement of rectangles. From these out-door vantage points there are fine views from the house's raised position over the Thames Valley.

25. Design for the piano corner of the living room, Kit's Close, Fawley Green, Oxfordshire, 1936

Pen, pencil, coloured crayon and office stamp on tracing paper (360 × 310)

Many of the walls in the dining, living and bedrooms had fitted shelving which in some cases, as shown in this drawing, curved cleanly around corners. The tops were covered with linoleum, an experiment used by other modern designers for desks and work surfaces, but one that did not prove enduring as the lino of the period was susceptible to permanent indentation from sharp objects. Fitted units were *de rigeur* for any modern house, and in this case Nicholson has even made the client's piano appear as part of the built-in look. The rather old-fashioned upright has been given a face-lift by the addition of a bentwood stool and jazzy rug.

26. Design for the north entrance front, Kit's Close, Fawley Green, Oxfordshire, *c*1936

Pencil, coloured stencil inks and Chinese white on tracing paper (400 × 520)

Hugh Casson's atmospheric drawing evokes the architecture of the Mediterranean. A ghostly couple approach the house up a drive planted with agave, the broad succulent green forms more dominant than the building itself. Except for the sharp outline of the house and its fenestration, it would appear that Casson has employed a soft ink and pencil technique, using a stencil brush, to conjure up this very un-English scene. And, in truth, the modernism of the architecture was foreign to many people.

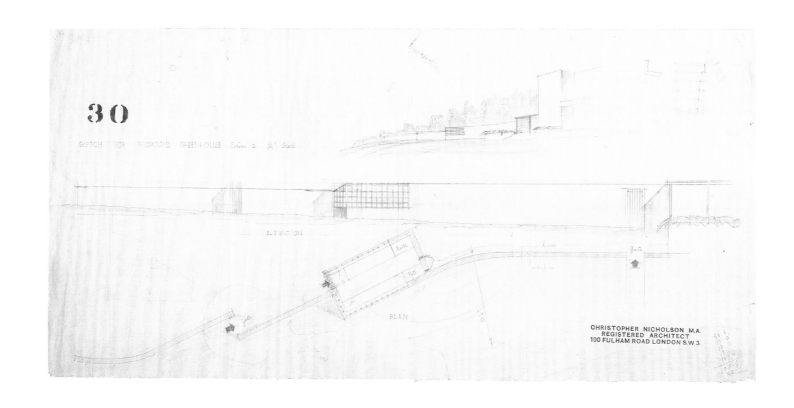

27. Design for a greenhouse, Kit's Close, Fawley Green, Oxfordshire, 1936

Pencil, green, red and blue crayon, stencil and office stamp on detail paper (360 × 755)

At Kit's Close, the greenhouse was cleverly integrated into the garden wall which protects the large kitchen garden behind from the winds bellowing across the valley. The greenhouse is frankly modern in design, repeating in the window pattern the strong grid pattern of the house. Sadly, because of its flimsy wooden construction, the greenhouse has not survived.

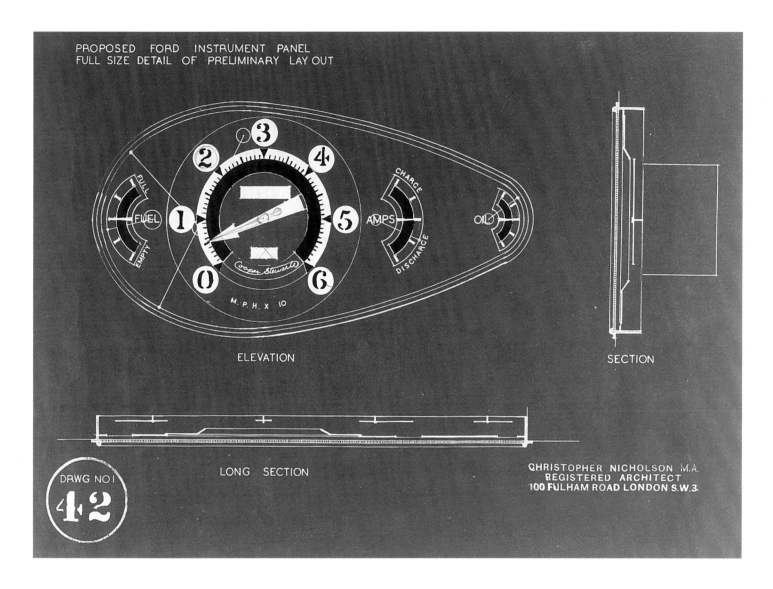

28. Design for an automobile instrument panel, for Cooper-Steward Engineering Co. Ltd, 1936
Blueprint with pencil, stencil and wash added (290 × 410)

This design for an instrument panel was not put into production. As a glider pilot and owner of fast cars, Nicholson took a keen interest in such gadgets because, especially in the air, his life depended on them. Cooper-Stewart Engineering Co. Ltd were manufacturers to the auto industry at the lower end of the market. During this period there were no new annual models, changes were made when necessary.

29. Design for a dining room, Dalingridge Farm, West Hoathly, West Sussex, for Miss Katia Freshfield, 1936

Pencil and coloured crayon on tracing paper (345 × 285)

Dalingridge Farm was a hybrid design – a small country house, its exterior basically traditional in style with two steeply pitched gables and windows pressed up under the eaves, but with a modern Nicholson interior. The client, Miss Freshfield, who specified the vernacular, lived in the house with her companion, Miss Prynne, until her death aged 91, in 1974. Most of the rooms had built-in units, similar to the sideboard and cupboards shown in this perspective. They were as plain as possible with flush doors and D-handles.

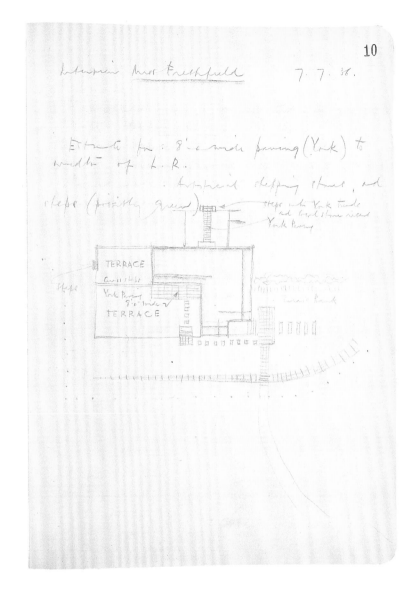

30. Preliminary design for exterior paving, Dalingridge Farm, West Hoathly, West Sussex, for Katia Freshfield, 1936

Blue carbon copy on page 10 of 'Reports 1' (250 × 180)

Nicholson kept small carbon copy notebooks for use on site visits and at interviews with clients. This sketch is on a page from one such report, and dates from the final design stage of Nicholson's work on Dalingridge Farm. Approval has been given by the client for the use of York stone paving to the principal walk and patio, and for artificial stone slabs for the rest of the grounds. Even in this freehand drawing Nicholson expresses the Cubist tendency of his architectural style. Although one suspects that Miss Freshfield planted a traditional English garden, it grew on a framework of modern design.

31. Design for Air House, Boyle Street, London, for the Royal Aeronautical Society, *c*1936

Black and coloured crayon and pencil (490 × 780), detail

With the growth of the aviation business in the 1930s, the membership of clubs and societies related to the many aspects of flight also increased. The most prestigious of these organisations was the Royal Aeronautical Society, which in 1936 attempted to purchase a Mayfair site for its new headquarters. This perspective shows Nicholson's building looming between the Georgian houses at the end of Old Burlington Street. The design was a near crib of Steel House in Tothill Street, by Burnet, Tait and Lorne, which had just been completed. The great height of the block was one reason for the abandonment of the scheme as the London County Council was against such over-scale development. Failing to gain the site, the Royal Aeronautical Society bought its present premises in Hamilton Place.

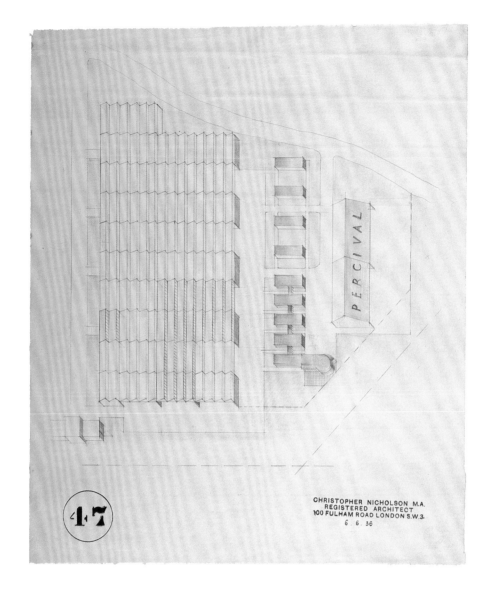

32. Design for the administration buildings and works factory for Percival Aircraft, Eaton Green Road, Luton, Bedfordshire, 1936

Pencil, coloured pencil, pen, stencil and office stamp on detail paper (530 × 450)

The Percival Aircraft Co. was founded in 1932 by Captain Edgar W Percival who had created a successful aeroplane manufacturing business on the strength of his three-seat touring monoplane, the Gull. In 1936, his works factory at Gravesend, Kent, was proving too small and as Luton Airport was about to open, Percival decided to move closer to the action. Taking up workshop accommodation in a two-bay hangar, Captain Percival commissioned Christopher Nicholson to design a large factory. It was not executed. This axonometric, appropriately looking down upon the works from the air, shows the orderly arrangement of assembly shed, administration blocks and hangar. The extended block in the lower right corner was to have been the reception area with an office for Captain Percival in the raised drum affording panoramic views of the factory and landing fields.

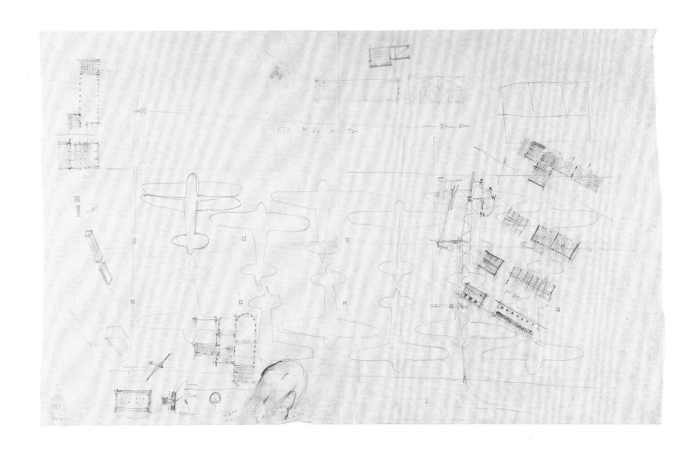

33. Preliminary study for the London Gliding Club, Dunstable, Bedfordshire, 1935

Pencil and red crayon on tracing paper (380 × 620)

Christopher Nicholson was able to combine two of his greatest passions, architecture and gliding, with his commission to design the London Gliding Club. This was Nicholson's own club, at the foot of the Dunstable Downs, where the previous accommodation for machines and members had been in old wooden huts. This sheet is crowded with Nicholson's first ideas. At the heart of the design, as it is in this drawing, is the hangar. Like a repeating wallpaper pattern, the red outlines of gliders interlock as Nicholson begins calculating the hangar dimensions. Some of the plans reveal that the architect contemplated designing the building in the shape of an aeroplane, a not uncommon configuration for airport buildings of the period as it made them easier to spot from the air.

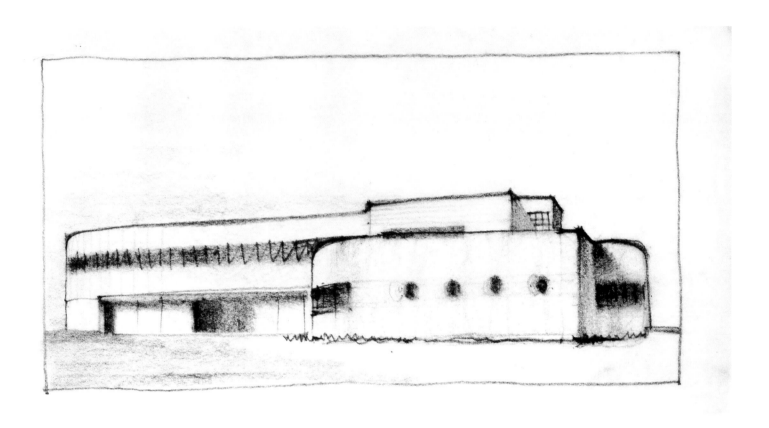

34. Preliminary design for the London Gliding Club, Dunstable, Bedfordshire, 1935

Pencil on tracing paper (255 × 120), detail

This confident pencil drawing is for the club almost as built. The only noticeable difference is for the wing with small porthole windows. This is the bar area, which when built was only half the size as shown here. The perspective is drawn from a low viewpoint so as to emphasise the massing of the foreground block beside the lightness of the receding block with its 60-foot open span for the hangar doors and the continuous band of windows overhead lighting the lounge and dining room.

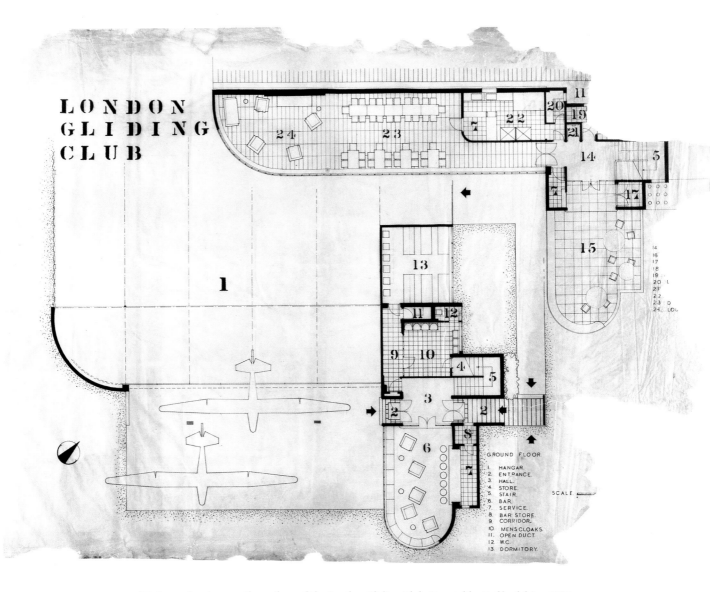

35. Ground and upper floor plans of the London Gliding Club, Dunstable, Bedfordshire, 1935

Pen and wash and stencil on tracing paper (725 × 1025, torn)

Two gliders stand sentry on the hangar apron in this damaged drawing. The missing labels for the numbered key to the upper floor are: 14. Landing, 15. Tea terrace, 16. Women's Lavatory (missing), 17. Chair store, 18. Lobby (torn from drawing), 19. Housemaid's closet, 20. Larder, 21. Telephone, 22. Kitchen, 23. Dining room, 24. Lounge

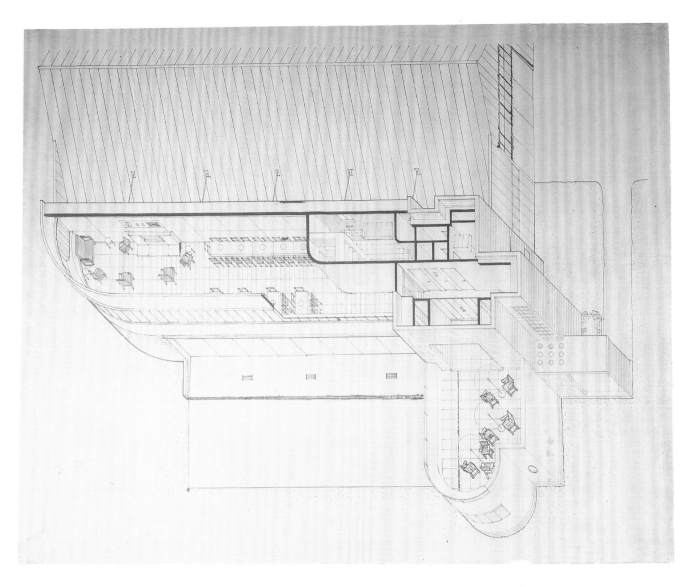

36. Axonometric of the London Gliding Club, Dunstable, Bedfordshire, 1936

Print with coloured washes added (695 × 880)

With their abstract qualities suited to the designs of modern architects, axonometrics became popular in the 1930s. Nicholson and Casson were enthusiastic exponents. They realised that such a seductive view would appeal to the club's members, glider pilots who would appreciate the sensation of sailing over the top of their roofless new building. The colour palette has been deliberately kept to a minimum, curiously highlighting only the brick, glass, furnishing fabric and kitchen walls. On the tea terrace, Nicholson has arranged the outdoor chairs of his own design which were just about to go on sale at Heal's.

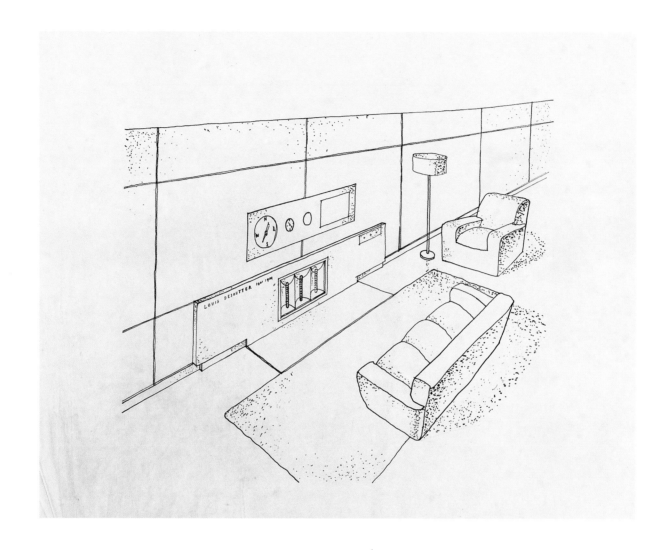

37. Design for the lounge fireplace, London Gliding Club, Dunstable, Bedfordshire, 1935

Pen and pencil on tracing paper (520 × 760), detail

Glider pilots sit for hours, and sometimes days, waiting for the right wind and weather conditions to allow them to soar. So it is not surprising that so much of Nicholson's clubhouse is taken up with bars and the restaurant and lounge. The seating around the fireplace is at the far end of the dining room, a long space with a continuous ribbon of windows curving at the lounge end giving uninterrupted views across the landing fields and Dunstable Downs. This is one of many variant designs for the lounge fireplace which Nicholson prepared. As in the finished design, the surround and floor slab are in travertine marble, and the electric fire in polished metal. But neither the memorial inscription to Louis Desoutter nor the direction indicator were added.

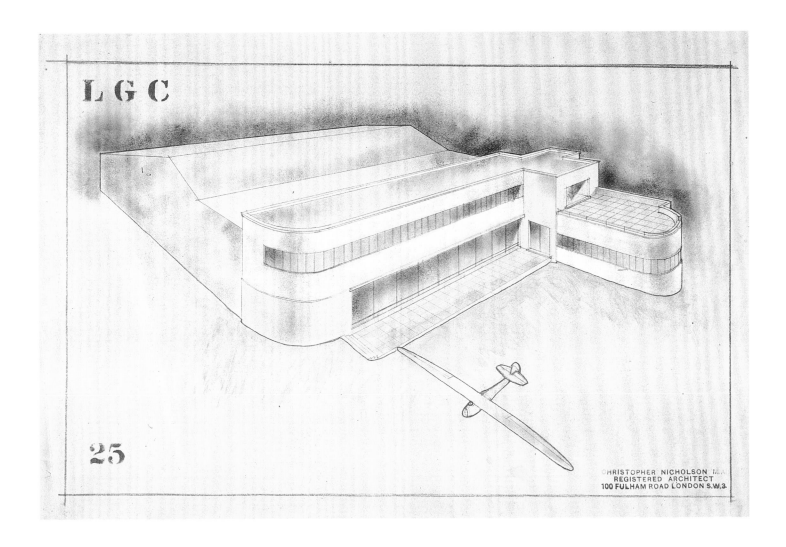

38. Design for the London Gliding Club, Dunstable, Bedfordshire, 1935

Pencil, coloured crayon, Chinese white, stencil and office stamp (480 × 720, approx)

When JM Richards reviewed Nicholson's gliding club in the pages of *The Architectural Review* in 1936, he drew upon the commonly perceived belief in the unity of technology and aesthetics held by the Modernists. 'It is only necessary', he wrote, 'to look at the scientific exactness of design, and to appreciate the formal beauty, of the advanced type of glider to recognise its affinity with the geometrical vocabulary of modern architecture.' Thus the prominence of the sailplanes in this drawing by Hugh Casson and in the famous Dell & Wainwright photograph which accompanied Richards's review.

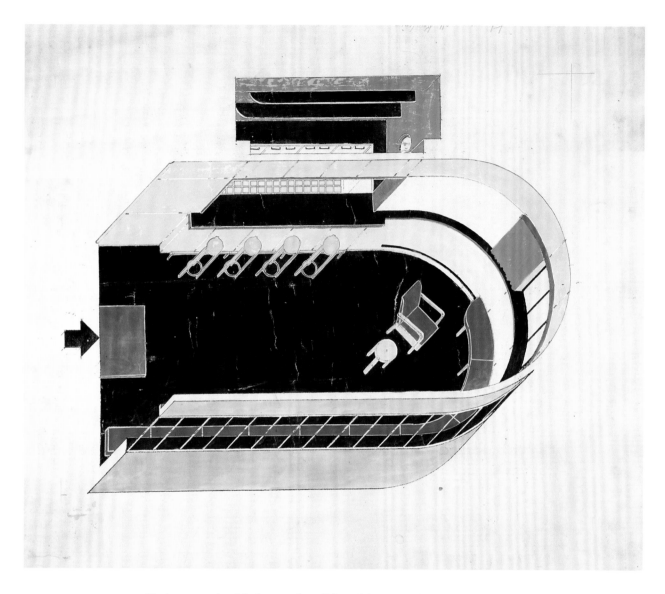

39. Axonometric of the bar, London Gliding Club, Dunstable, Bedfordshire, 1936

Pencil, pen, gouache and Chinese white (400 × 400, approx), detail

Hugh Casson joined his former Cambridge teacher on a full-time basis when the London Gliding Club commission came into Nicholson's office. It was Casson who created this striking axonometric of the semicircular-ended bar which occupies the ground floor wing alongside the apron to the hangar. Nicholson's wife, the designer and painter EQ, was responsible for the interior decoration of the club including the choice of colours. To furnish the bar they chose Aalto stools, which were being imported into Britain from Finland by Finmar. Throughout the club, EQ used light colours, except for the bar, which she had painted in deep shades of blue and reddish-brown. This drawing also shows the light green colouring of the external rendering, which was considered a novel change from the white and cream of most other Modernist buildings of the period.

40. Design for alterations and additions to 25 Godfrey Street, Kensington and Chelsea, London, for FHL Searl, 1937

Pencil, coloured crayon and Chinese white on detail paper (405 × 250)

This small mid-nineteenth century terrace house, tucked-in behind the King's Road, would have been transformed into a fashionable pied-à-terre for a bachelor had it been built. The job involved stripping the original stucco-render and refacing the front with bricks. Long horizontal windows, of the sliding type on the first floor, would have replaced the old single vertical sash openings. A vestigial concrete canopy would have sheltered the front door, while a large floating canopy was envisaged sailing over the balcony of the new top floor, extending out from 'the own bedroom', as it says on the plan.

MARS GROUP EXHIBITION

CHRISTOPHER NICHOLSON M.A.
REGISTERED ARCHITECT
100 FULHAM ROAD LONDON S.W.3.

41. Design for the Garden Landscape section, MARS Group Exhibition, New Burlington Galleries, Burlington Gardens, London, 1937

Pencil, pen, Chinese white, green and blue crayon on tracing paper (465 × 630)

Le Corbusier wrote of the 1938 MARS (Modern Architectural Research) Group exhibition: 'On January 19th I dropped out of an aeroplane [which Nicholson would have appreciated] into the midst of a charming demonstration of youth, which revealed the architecture of tomorrow to be as stimulating as it is self-reliant.' The theme was 'Elements of Modern Architecture' and Nicholson was in charge of the garden landscape section. To create an outdoor room so that 'house and garden coalesce', as it proclaimed on a large caption,

Nicholson erected a pergola of four tapering fins enclosing a silver birch tree, a concrete-ringed plot of grass, and suspended on the back brick wall, a plant container. A large photomural on the end wall showed an aerial view of Lubetkin's weekend house on the Dunstable Downs, only a few minutes flight from Nicholson's own gliding club. Hugh Casson assisted Nicholson on this major modern exhibition, and thus this work is a design precursor to the Casson-directed 1951 Festival of Britain.

CHRISTOPHER NICHOLSON M.A.
REGISTERED ARCHITECT
100 FULHAM ROAD LONDON S.W.3.

42. Preliminary design for plywood armchair for Isokon, 1937

Pencil, red pencil and stencil on detail paper (430 × 680)

Nicholson designed this armchair for his friend Jack Pritchard whose furniture company, Isokon, specialised in bending and moulding plywood into adventurous new shapes. This chair bears comparison with Nicholson's section for the MARS Exhibition which he was designing at the same time; both the canopy over the display and the chair are manufactured out of curved ply pierced by holes – the circle and globe a fashionable motif of the moment. The legs of the chair, not shown in this drawing, were of bent plywood snaking up as supports below the broad arms and centre of the seat. The chair did not go into production.

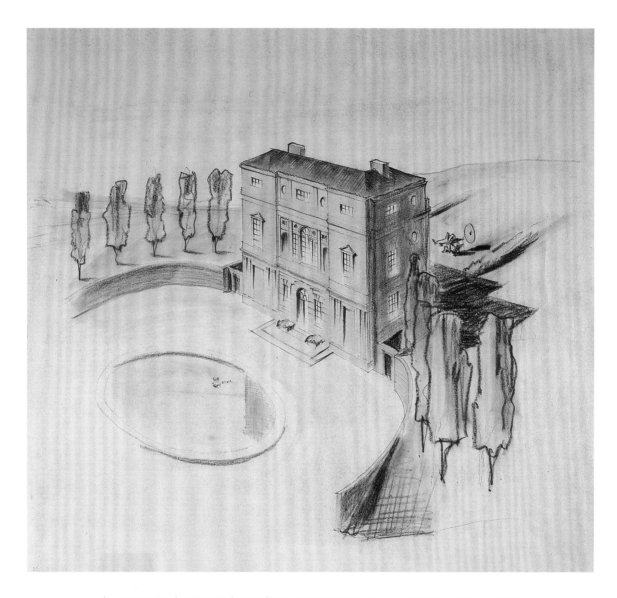

43. Design for the front of the Pantheon, West Dean, West Sussex, for Edward James, 1938
Print with blue, green and yellow crayon, black pastel, brown wash and pencil (450 × 480)

The Pantheon, like Monkton, was to have been another surrealist creation for Edward James. In 1937 James purchased the facade of the Pantheon – once a popular, London assembly hall designed by James Wyatt between 1769 and 1772, which stood in Oxford Street at the south-west corner of Poland Street. Each stone of the facade had been numbered before dismantling, with the view to re-erection on James's Sussex estate. As this perspective shows, the approach up the drive would have led visitors to believe that they were about to enter the staid gentility of a Georgian country house. But in this drawing by Casson, the sun-worshipping figures lounging in the garden hint at the unexpectedly modern world that was to lie behind.

44. Design model, with added figures by John Piper, showing the rear of the Pantheon, West Dean, West Sussex, for Edward James, 1938

Photograph with coloured gouache added (440 × 560)

Nicholson had a plaster-covered model made of his design for the Pantheon. This was then photographed so that the artist John Piper could add a row of caryatids on the rear elevation. These would have been constructed of sheet metal if the house had been built. Piper's Easter Island figures were a fanciful interpretation of a classical precedent, capturing the clashing hybrid mood of this unbuilt scheme. And, in contrast to the light-hearted drawings by Casson, this rather sinister photographic image for the house better reflected the client's disquieting surrealist personality, embedded as it was in the current psychoanalytical world of Freudian neurosis.

45. Design for the terrace for the Pantheon, West Dean, West Sussex, for Edward James, 1938
Pencil and coloured crayon on tracing paper, mounted (215 × 295)

The rear of the Pantheon turned its back on the old. Nicholson's design was fresh and clear. In this perspective by Casson, the folding windows of the dining room are partially folded back. Privacy to the outer rooms was to have been obtained by the vertical slabs dividing the corridor windows. The screen of caryatids played a transitional role between the classical front and modern back of the house, their status having been legitimised in progressive architec-

ture by their use in the entrance porch of Lubetkin's Highpoint II. Another outdoor terrace was planned within the large central well of the house, and would have given views through the elegant Palladian window of the salvaged Pantheon facade. As the War intervened, the house was never built. The stones of London's Pantheon are believed to have been broken up and re-used as building hardcore.

46. Design for the living room for the Pantheon, West Dean, West Sussex, for Edward James, 1938
Pencil, coloured crayon and Chinese white on tracing paper, mounted (195 × 295)

The Pantheon would have been more a showcase for Edward James's surrealist collection than Monkton House, which was a surrealist work in itself. At Monkton, James had asked Nicholson and Casson to design the living room like the insides of an unhealthy dog, panting in an uneven way. The architects, thus inspired, worked out a system of walls made of rubber sheets which contracted and expanded irregularly by means of compressed air jets. It was not put into operation. At the Pantheon, the living room was to have been sedate in comparison. There were surrealist touches, like the bear-skin rug hung on the chimney breast instead of laying in front of it, and cult objects like the African sculpted head mirroring the primitivism which pervaded the client's life. In 1939, James moved to the States and then to the heat of the Mexican jungle where he spent the remainder of his life hand-building a concrete fantasy.

47. Competition design for a weekend cottage, 1938

Pencil and coloured crayon on tracing paper, mounted (200 × 305)

As a publicity stunt, the writer and interior designer, Arundell Clarke, invited a select group of architects to submit designs for a weekend cottage. Although not strictly a competition, at the cocktail party given by Clarke in October 1938 for the architects and press, all the designs were exhibited and the model by Le Corbusier and Clive Entwistle acclaimed the winner. A prerequisite of the brief had been that the cottage blend with the landscape, not only as an aesthetic consideration but, in the event of an air raid, as a camouflage tactic; the winning entry had a flat roof covered in grass. Nicholson's submission, seen here in a perspective by Casson, relied on deep sheltering eaves to make it less conspicuous from the air. The house proved to be prophetic – Casson was to spend most of the approaching War as a camouflage specialist, hiding military installations from enemy air surveillance.

48. Competition design for a weekend cottage, 1938

Pencil and brown, blue and green crayon on tracing paper, mounted (145 × 190)

This perspective by Casson slices through the floor to ceiling window of the living room, creating the illusion that there is no distinction between inside and out. Nicholson's design was created on the eve of the War and stands at a stylistic crossroad in Modernism. It could well be a house built after the War, in the 1950s. The expression of concern for space, light and rigorous proportioning is by now a standard expression. But the fair-faced brick and exposed ceiling beams anticipate the return to natural building materials. The use of a sloping monopitch roof was to be popularised in post-war houses by the likes of Arne Jacobsen and Marcel Breuer.

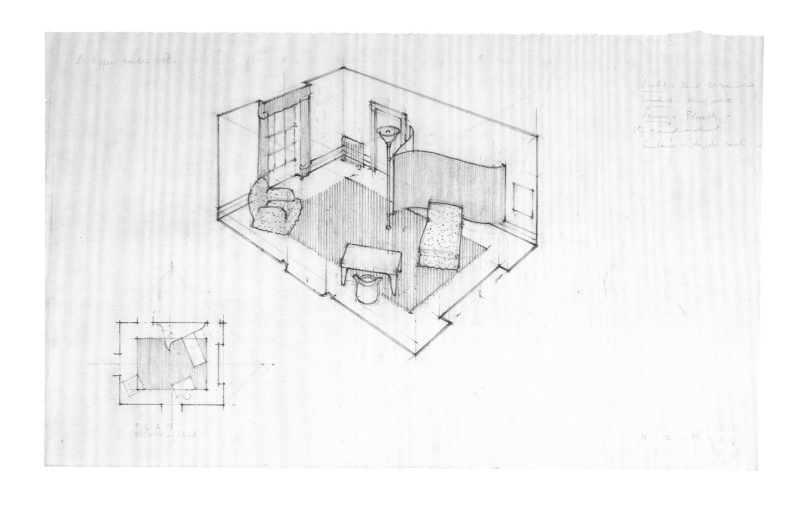

49. Design for consulting room, 4 Upper Harley Street, London, for Rosemary Pritchard, 1938

Pencil and red crayon (260 × 435)

Rosemary, known as Molly to her friends, was the wife of Jack Pritchard, founder of the modern furniture company Isokon. As a psychologist, she specialised in personality testing. In this cut-away perspective of her consulting room, two walls have been removed to allow us to spy into the intimate world of doctor and patient. The design has a sense of professional feminine calm about it, enhanced by the loose-covered armchair and couch – a man would have had leather – and the curtains in a dyed coral, as it says in the upper right corner of the drawing. The carpet, sensibly and aesthetically, is sunk flush with the flooring. Dr Pritchard's desk is of moulded plywood by her husband's firm. The curving screen is Nicholson's design, made of flexoply stained grained walnut and pivoted on an uplighter already in the client's possession. The screen afforded privacy for the reclining patient and needed storage space behind.

50. Illustration of the properties of weather fronts, 1939

Red, blue and black washes, pen and red crayon on newspaper tipped into notebook (230 × 605)

Nicholson's sense of artistic experimentation touched every aspect of his life. In 1939, he joined the Royal Naval Volunteer Reserve and was commissioned a lieutenant. To his great satisfaction, he landed a position as a meteorological officer and was sent for training to Ditton Park, near Slough. His notebook, from which this illustration is taken, is filled with colourful diagrams and intensive training data on weather and atmospheric conditions. Lacking a large sheet of paper, Nicholson improvised, neatly tearing a strip from a page of *The Daily Telegraph* and *Morning Post*, and brushed on a drawing of a weather front, appropriately colouring the warm air red and the cold in blue.

51. Preliminary design for a house, Borough Green, Kent, for Commander Stephen Banks, 1946

Pencil and red wash over wax (125 × 240)

The client's wife, Eliza Banks, was Christopher Nicholson's younger half-sister. She describes this scheme as the dream house that never came true. It was to have been built on a property they owned in Kent. Nicholson, recently out of the Forces, had time on his hands to work out the scheme in great detail, making many sketch designs. One was this playful elevation created by first drawing in wax and then covering the sheet in the coloured wash which does not adhere to the non-absorbent wax surface. The design is similar to Nicholson's previous house project, made before the war, for a weekend bungalow with a monopitch roof. In this drawing, the large row of dining room windows overlooks a terrace which was to have been covered in a giant flower box. For many years after the war, with social housing the priority, permission to build private houses was hard to obtain.

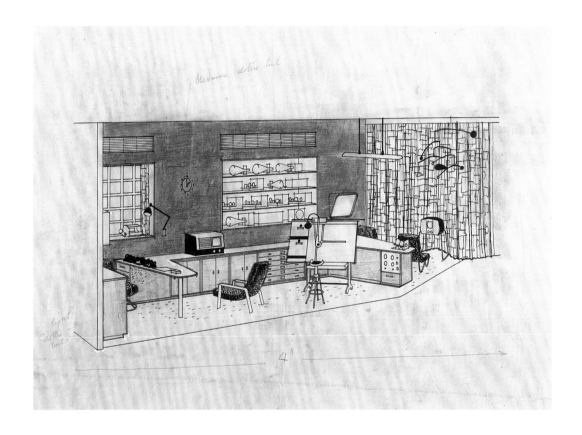

52. Design for television research engineer's office for the 'Britain Can Make It' exhibition, Victoria & Albert Museum, London, 1946

Pen and wash, pencil, blue crayon, and Chinese white on tracing paper (620 × 750), detail

In 1946, hundreds of thousands of design-hungry visitors queued to see the 'Britain Can Make It' exhibition, daydreaming about a bright new future of homes and offices filled with desirable objects. Nicholson and Casson's design for an office for a television research engineer was not a stuffy and sterile laboratory but a stylish executive suite, furnished with abstract patterned curtains, a Calder-inspired mobile and comfortable modern furniture. The recessed shelving displayed cathode-ray tubes and television chassis. The latest technology was at the engineer's fingertips – a dictaphone resting on the window shelf, a control panel of knobs and switches, and located in this drawing above the drawing table, a mock-up experimental television projector. Two of Nicholson's latest televisions for Ferranti were the obvious stars of the setting – a table model and a console set.

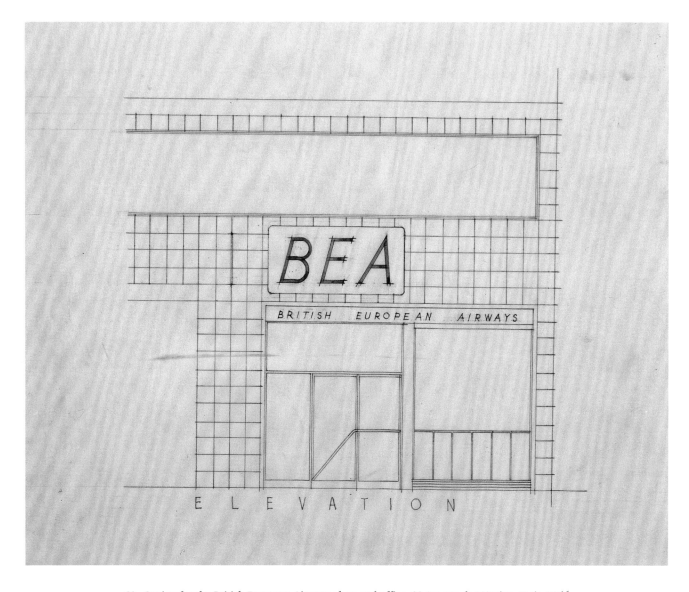

53. Design for the British European Airways shop and office, 38 Avenue de L'Opéra, Paris, 1946
Black and red pen and pencil on tracing paper (560 × 750), detail

The London-Paris route was a major run for BEA. Nicholson's shop and office for the airline in the French capital was on Haussman's chic Avenue de L'Opéra, and certainly showed that the British could maintain a high standard of design in the face of so much surrounding elegance. A grid of glass bricks patterned the facade. The diagonal line of the entrance door handle was a single eccentricity breaking the rigidity of the grid. Behind the long ribbon window on the first floor were the offices of the manager and secretary.

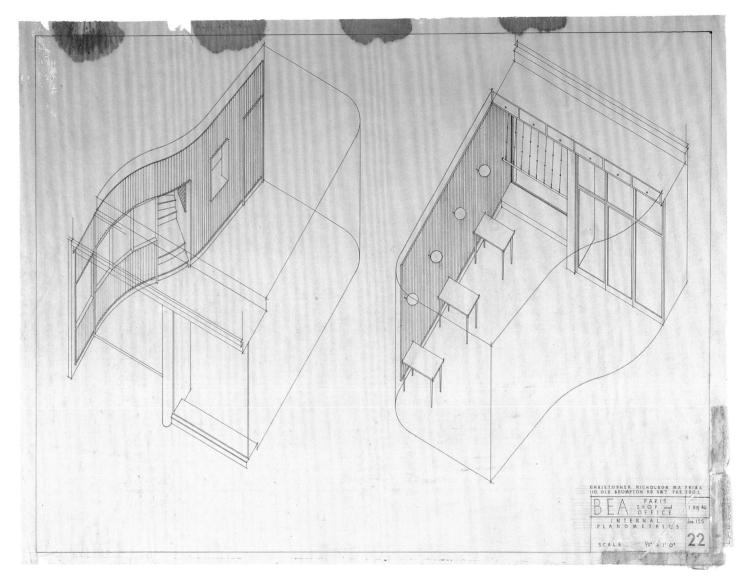

54. Design for the British European Airways shop and office, 38 Avenue de L'Opéra, Paris, 1946

Black and red pen and pencil on tracing paper (500 × 745)

The two projections in this drawing are internal planometrics, and as such are labelled. The planometric is a rarely used form of axonometric, which by its nature always gives the plan in true scale. By maintaining a thin outline of the edges of the office, Nicholson has avoided the necessity of either covering over or cutting away the walls, commonly the case in most axonometric drawings. He is thus able to show the curvature of the walls which in fact mask the ordinary rectangular plan of the given site. Within the wall shown in the left planometric are display windows, staircase entrance and cashier's grille. The other projection illustrates the reception area with its vertical timber boarding, four wall lights and simple tables. At the window is suspended an open half-screen made of wires and decorative metal balls. The display space below was left free for posters mounted on frames.

55. Design for air terminal at St Enoch's Station, Glasgow, for British European Airways, 1947

Pen, pencil, Chinese white, pastel and yellow wash on tracing paper (240 × 400), detail

This jolly perspective by Hugh Casson is for redesigning the BEA offices on the concourse of St Enoch's station in Glasgow as a sophisticated air terminal. Passengers could begin their journey with the airline at this central city location before being whisked by a BEA coach to the airport. Three counters ringed the waiting room: an information booth, a booking office, and a traffic desk for check-in where not only the luggage was weighed but the passenger too. In 1947, it was possible to fly from Glasgow on BEA to Aberdeen, Belfast, Inverness, Orkney, Shetland, Stornoway, Tiree, Wick and, for a princely £12.10s., to London.

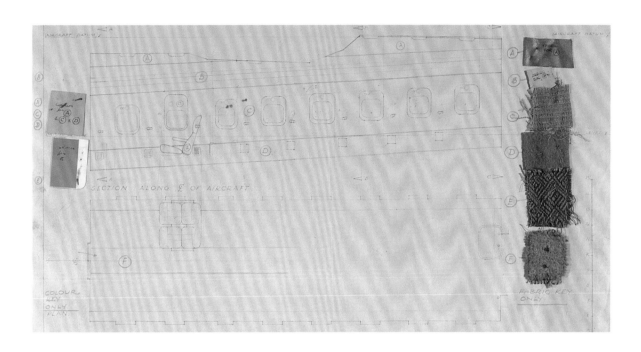

56. Key for colours and fabrics for the interior of the Bristol Wayfarer aeroplane, for British European Airways, 1946

Print with red crayon and pen added and samples attached (640 × 610), detail

The sombre colours of the war years persisted in dominating fashions and furnishings in its aftermath. Thus the whole of Nicholson's scheme for the main passenger saloon of the Wayfarer was in shades of grey, only relieved by the red of the carpet. (The sample fabric for the carpet, the bottom swatch on the right labelled 'F', is not the correct shade as materials such as dyes were notoriously difficult to obtain.) Most of the suggested fabrics were of man-made fibres. The cabin walls ('C') and seats ('E'), for example, were to be covered in spun nylon and woven by Edinburgh Weavers, a leading firm of fashion textiles manufacturers.

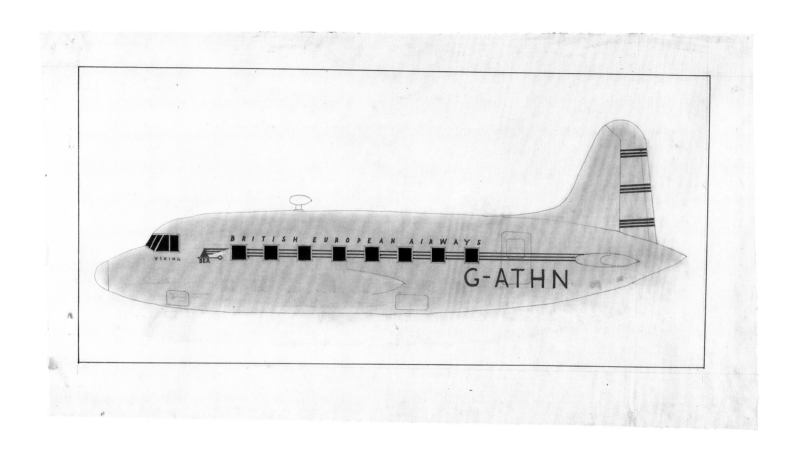

57.   Design for livery for the Vickers Viking aeroplane, for British European Airways, 1947

Pen, pencil, red pen, grey, black and red washes and Chinese white on tracing paper (255 × 495)

The design for the Vickers Viking, which formed the main core of BEA's first fleet of aircraft, had been based on the Wellington Bomber. The early Vikings were 21-seaters; Nicholson had the job of developing the livery, interior design and colour scheme for the next version, the 34-seater. In this suggested design for the exterior decoration, he stretched the triple lines of the BEA flying key into strips running the length of the aircraft body. The registration is fictitious, although BEA's letters always began with 'G'. In this drawing, Nicholson has printed the aeroplane type under the cockpit windows, the usual position for the plane's name. All the Vikings flown by BEA were given names beginning with the letter 'V', giving rise to such examples as Vampire, Valerie, Vivacious and Votary.

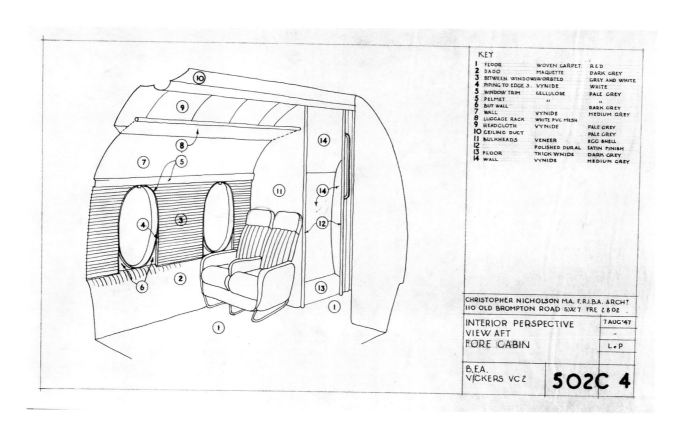

KEY

1	FLOOR	WOVEN CARPET	RED
2	DADO	MAQUETTE	DARK GREY
3	BETWEEN WINDOWS	WORSTED	GREY AND WHITE
4	PIPING TO EDGE 3.	VYNIDE	WHITE
5	WINDOW TRIM	CELLULOSE	PALE GREY
6	PELMET	"	"
	BUT WALL		DARK GREY
7	WALL	VYNIDE	MEDIUM GREY
8	LUGGAGE RACK	WHITE PVC MESH	
9	HEADCLOTH	VYNIDE	PALE GREY
10	CEILING DUCT		PALE GREY
11	BULKHEADS	VENEER	EGG SHELL
12		POLISHED DURAL	SATIN FINISH
13	FLOOR	THICK VYNIDE	DARK GREY
14	WALL	VYNIDE	MEDIUM GREY

CHRISTOPHER NICHOLSON M.A. F.R.I.B.A. ARCHT
110 OLD BROMPTON ROAD S.W.7 FRE 2802.

INTERIOR PERSPECTIVE
VIEW AFT
FORE CABIN

7 AUG '47

—

L . P

B.E.A.
VICKERS VC2

502C 4

58. Design for interior finishes for the Vickers VC2 aeroplane, for British European Airways, 1947

Pen, pencil and stencil on tracing paper (305 × 445), detail

The Vickers VC2 was another aircraft mooted by BEA for production but never taken up. Eventually, it developed into the famous Vickers Viscount. The great feature of the VC2 was to have been the large elliptical windows. Nicholson prepared designs for the aircraft's livery and interior finishes and furnishings. As indicated by the key, many materials were to be man-made and in the BEA colours.

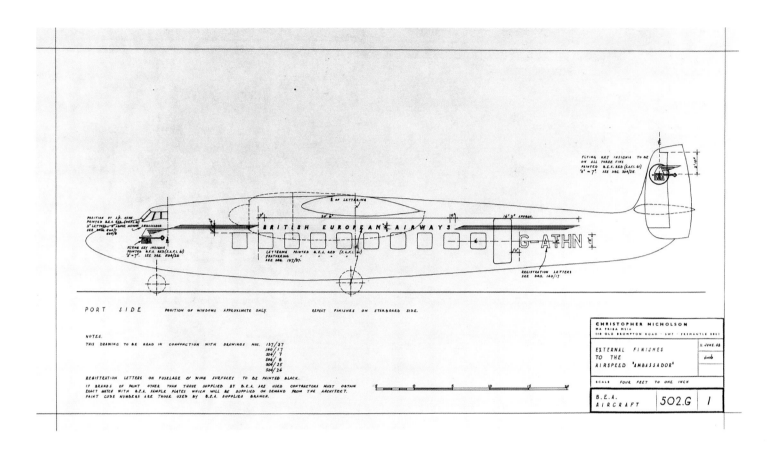

59. Design for livery for the Airspeed Ambassador aeroplane, for British European Airways, 1948

Pen and office stamp on tracing paper (330 × 595)

Arranging the placement of the BEA logo and lettering on the Airspeed Ambassador was one of the last jobs Nicholson undertook before he made his fateful trip to Switzerland for the International Gliding Championship. The Airspeed Ambassador did not go into production with BEA and developed into the Elizabethan class, so named in honour of the new Queen who ascended to the throne in 1951. By that time, BEA had replaced its 'flying key' insignia with a coat-of-arms.

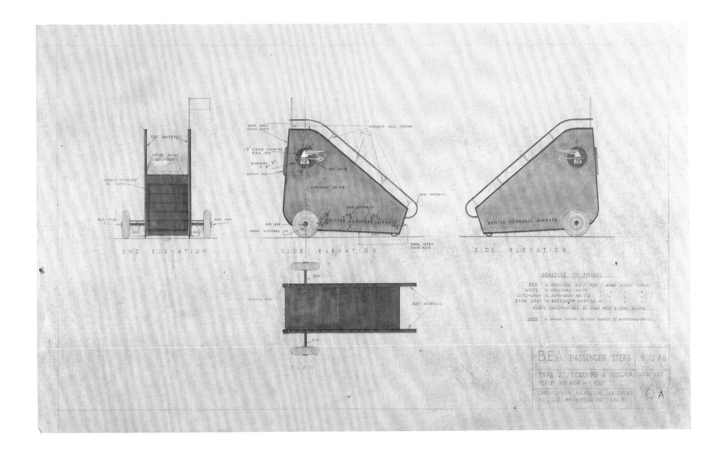

60. Design for livery for passenger steps for British European Airways, 1946

Print with grey and red washes, Chinese white and pencil added (365 × 610)

Before manned flight, stairs were the only way to reach the heavens. For the embarking air traveller, the rolling steps placed on the runway alongside the aeroplane herald the last contact with the safety of the earth; for the nervous flyer, they are as significant as an ascent to the guillotine. Nicholson took immense pains to completely wrap these BEA steps in the airline's company colours. Even the wheel hubs and axles received a coat of the standard BEA hard glossy red paint finish.

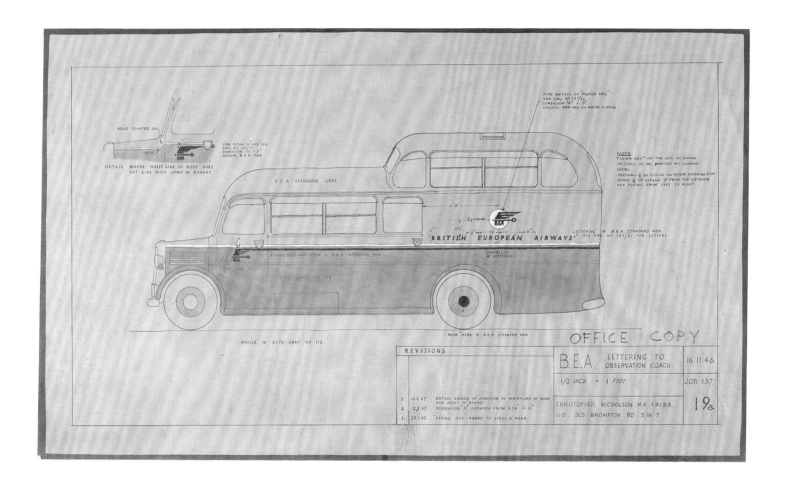

61. Design for livery for an observation coach, for British European Airways, 1946

Print with grey and red washes, Chinese white and pencil added (305 × 515)

After checking-in at the city terminal, the sense of adventure and novelty associated with flight continued for passengers as they stepped aboard this observation coach to take them to the airport. The raised section of the vehicle served two purposes: the obvious one of allowing passengers a raised forward view, and also more practically, the creation of a large space below for stowing luggage. Nicholson has emphasised this above and below world by vertically dividing the coach with two shades of BEA grey, with the equator line a white painted architectural moulding – a 'bead' as it says on the upper left detail on this drawing.

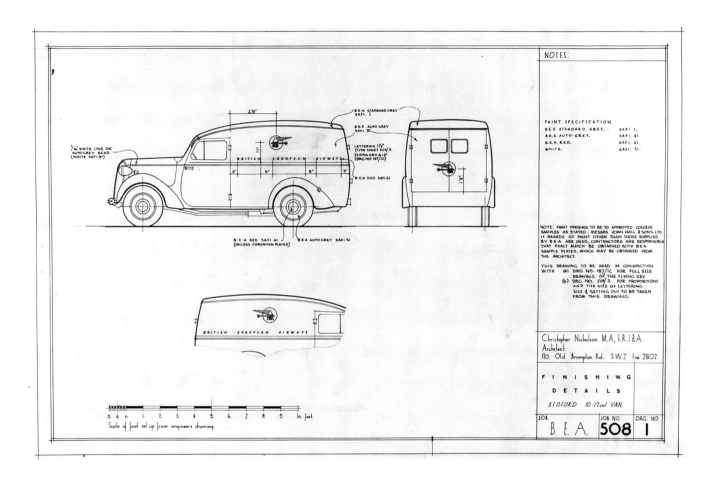

62. Design for livery for a Bedford van, for British European Airways, 1947

Pen, pencil and stencil on tracing paper (345 × 530)

Nothing is left to chance on this finely drawn sheet for colouring and detailing a Bedford van for the BEA land fleet. Even the reverse side of the vehicle is detailed in a cropped elevation so that the painter has no leeway for error. The execution of the careful line and hand-lettering is an achievement of great skill; the drawn scale is of technical beauty.

63. Design for travelling exhibition trailer for British European Airways, 1948

Pencil, red and black pen, grey and red washes, red crayon, white pastel and Chinese white on tracing paper (235 × 520)

Nicholson transformed the chassis of a Tasker Andover trailer into a touring advertisement for BEA. Arriving on site, the liveried driver flicked back the high-level covered box which ran the whole length of one side of the trailer and withdrew an awning for sheltering the queue of visitors. He then swung back the folding doors and popped out the stairs and handrail. Within was displayed an exhibition of hope – world travel, which only a few years previously had been tinged with the fear of war.

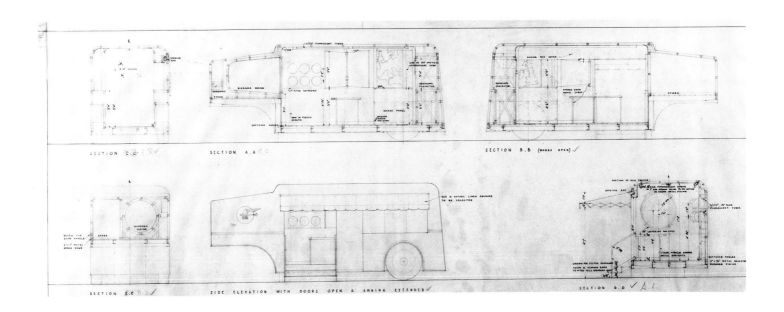

64. Plan of travelling exhibition trailer for British European Airways, 1948

Pen, pencil, red crayon and stencil (735 × 990), detail

The visitor to the BEA exhibition was treated to the practical and fantasy aspects of a new world airline. To create a dreamy atmosphere, the interior was dimly lit and set whirling by an optical illumination from a projector. After the introductory panel came a series of maps showing flight routes, then panels about moving freight by air, and small models of the BEA aircraft set into perspex globes. As a finale there was a diorama of an interior of a passenger plane, a miniature mock-up probably of one of Nicholson's own designs.

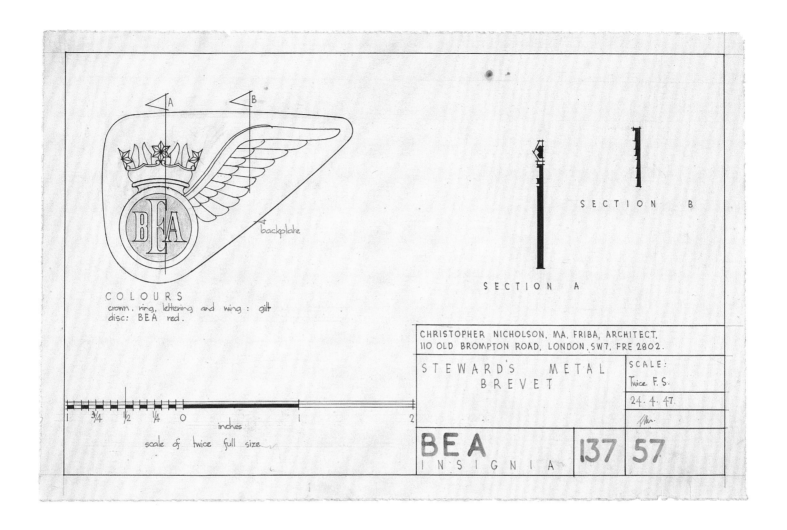

COLOURS
crown, ring, lettering and wing : gilt
disc: BEA red.

SECTION B

SECTION A

CHRISTOPHER NICHOLSON, MA, FRIBA, ARCHITECT,
110 OLD BROMPTON ROAD, LONDON, SW7, FRE 2802.

STEWARD'S METAL
BREVET

SCALE:
Twice F.S.

24.4.47.

BEA
INSIGNIA

137 57

inches

scale of twice full size

65. Design for air steward's brevet, for British European Airways, 1947

Black and brown pen, brown stencil, red crayon and pencil on detail paper (200 x 305)

An assistant in Nicholson's office has drawn this piece of insignia by showing the intricate cuts in two sections, applying the same care and detail as a classical architect would treat a drawing for an entablature. The single wing designates a member of the cabin crew. The crown was used only for a short period by BEA before the corporate logo changed to a coat-of-arms.

view from north east

66. Design for Coln Hatherop and Quenington village centre, Gloucestershire, 1946-47

Pen, pencil, coloured pastel and Chinese white (250 × 305), detail

Sir Thomas Bazley, for whom Nicholson had worked at the beginning of his career, asked his friend to return to Gloucestershire and design a community centre to serve the villages surrounding his country estate. Nicholson's village centre was to have been in the modern idiom of Gropius and Fry's Impington College in Cambridgeshire. Nicholson even procured a set of drawings for this famous pre-war scheme. In this perspective by Casson, the speeding car is approaching the part of the building containing the large hall, with its tall windows encased in concrete surrounds. Although Nicholson got as far as designing the furniture – in the style of Ernest Race, painted white with vermilion upholstery – the co-operating villages never raised the necessary funds and the centre was not built.

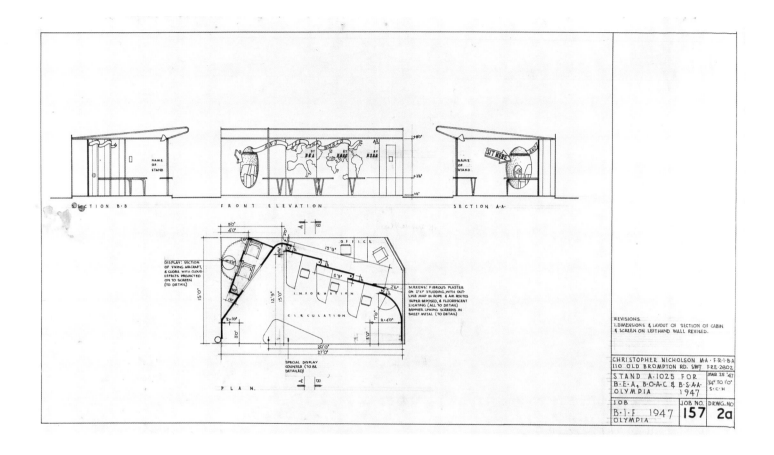

67. Design for stand for BEA, BOAC and BSAA, British Industries Fair, Olympia Exhibition Hall, London, 1947

Pen, red pen, pencil and stencil on tracing paper (380 × 680)

The three major airlines in post-war Britain combined forces in this exhibition stand. With tongue-in-cheek, a big arrow invited the visitor to step into a small section of a Vickers Viking aeroplane, sit down and wistfully stare into a screen disguised as a port-hole window with cloud effects projected onto it. A sheet metal banner unfurled across the top of a world map, portioned up between British European Airways for the Continent and British Overseas Airways Company for the rest of the globe except the Latin world served by British South American Airways. The outline of the continents was a twisting length of rope.

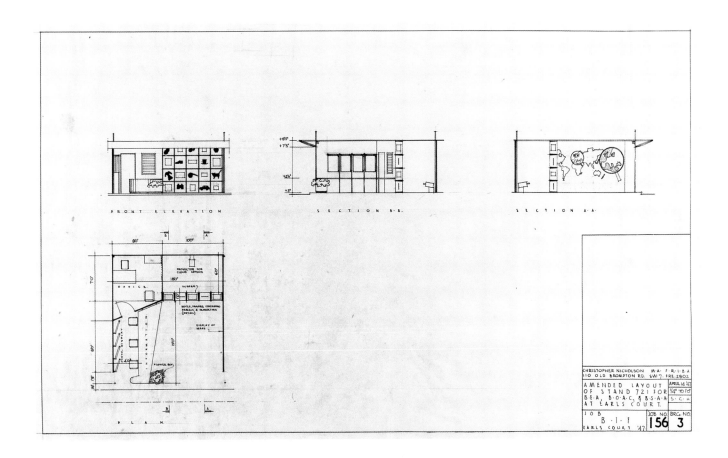

68. Design for cargo freight exhibition stand, British Industries Fair, Earls Court Exhibition Hall, London, 1947

Pencil, pen and red pen on tracing paper (420 × 690)

The clients for this exhibition stand were British European Airways, British Overseas Airways and British South American Airways. Combined, these three airlines covered most of the major world routes, as the map on the side wall indicates. The stand promoted air freight. At the rear, Nicholson stacked a bank of perspex boxes, alternating illustrations of examples of cargo items painted onto the perspex, with actual objects like newspapers, hearing aids and containers of penicillin. The whole display wall was then set in motion by swirling clouds, illuminated from behind by a hidden projector. The reception desk, in the shape of an aeroplane wing, was covered in corrugated aluminium. A small flower box prevented the visitor standing at the desk from toppling off the stand.

69. Design for stand, Ideal Home Exhibition, for Arthur Sanderson & Sons Ltd, Olympia, London, 1948

Pencil, pastel and Chinese white on tracing paper (380 × 465), detail

Hugh Casson is always in his element when drawing exhibition architecture. His quick and lively sketching technique evokes the frivolous enjoyment of the fair; his people are as important as the architecture. The women are attired in smart outfits as colourful as Sanderson's display of fabrics and wallpapers. Post-war austerity has evaporated.

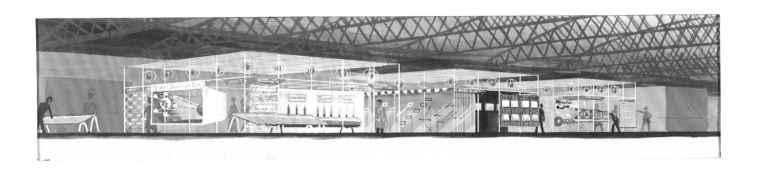

70. Design for exhibition stand, British Industries Fair, for British Tube Investments Ltd., Birmingham, *c*1948

Gouache and Chinese white (225 × 490), detail

This design for an exhibition stand is a key work in Casson's development leading to the 1951 Festival of Britain of which he was Director of Architecture. Much of the Festival's vocabulary of effects is here; principal amongst these are the use of a transparent enclosure and the decorative theme of the molecular structure. The stand is made of a light-weight metal frame, drawn here in finely ruled lines of Chinese white. The display panels are clipped onto this framework in an ordered randomness. Much of the Festival architecture was similarly conceived, not as a series of buildings but as skeletal shelters for the public to weave through.

71. Design for exhibition stand, British Industries Fair, for Carnegie Chemicals Ltd, *c*1948

Pencil, pastel and Chinese white on tracing paper (235 × 290), detail

A curving wall of large coloured balls, presumably representing chemical molecules, presages the molecular screen designed by Edward Mills for the South Bank site of the 1951 Festival of Britain. The detonation of the atom bomb during the closing months of the Second World War had quickened the public's imagination, impressing upon them that the scientific exploitation of the smallest particle then known to man could create the most powerful impact upon nature. Designers translated the fearsome into the decorative. Here, in Casson's perspective, the composition of a chemical cocktail is rendered as harmless as a patterned curtain.

72. Design for alterations and additions to the Ward Room, HMS *Daedalus*, Lee-on-Solent, Hampshire, 1947

Pen, pencil, red crayon and Chinese white on tracing paper (295 × 385)

Nicholson had spent part of the War stationed at the Lee-on-Solvent naval base, just outside Portsmouth, an establishment which had opened in 1918 as the Royal Naval Air Service Seaplane School. Nicholson's alterations to the Ward Room were more in the way of a refurbishment than structural. In this perspective by Casson, Nicholson's design for a large screen to hide the service entrance can be seen at the end of the room; it is covered in the criss-cross lines of studded quilted leather. The chandeliers and table lights, with small red shades, are derived from the most famous officers' mess of all, the Painted Hall in the Royal Naval Hospital, Greenwich.

aerial view

73. Design for a civil air centre, 1947
Print (305 × 470)

After the War, Nicholson was appointed as the architectural consultant to a committee set up to advise the Air Minister on the administration of private aviation. The chairman of the investigation committee was Whitney Straight, who before the War had established a company to help design and operate new airports in conjunction with local authorities. The Straight Corporation had been responsible for many of Britain's first municipal airports, such as Ramsgate, Ipswich and Exeter, all with well-designed buildings by progressive architects. Nicholson, having spent much of his war career in running air bases, was well versed in the art of airport design.

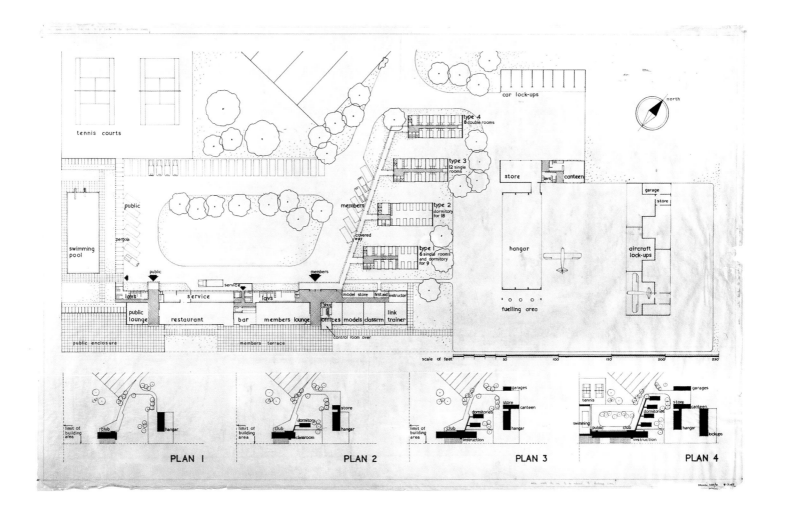

74. Plans for a civil air centre, 1947

Pen and wash, pencil and stencil on tracing paper (665 × 1040)

The term 'civil' attached to a private air club seems an anomaly until one considers that during the war years no civilian airports were allowed to operate. Nicholson's theoretical design, created for a government report, was to have been like a holiday camp for flyers. The small plans at the bottom of the sheet illustrate the potential growth of a site from a single club building and hangar to a full-blown holiday centre. It is obvious that the idea was to have lots of these centres scattered around the country. Members could thus jump in their aeroplanes, fly off to one of these airport clubs, check into a dormitory (this centre sleeps sixty-five) and then dine and drink the night away in the comfortable restaurant and lounge. Unlike those fantastic ideas of flight from science fiction that have come true, it seems peculiar that Nicholson's practical scheme for private airport resorts did not.

97

75. Design for experimental structures laboratory, Wexham Springs, Buckinghamshire, for the Cement and Concrete Association Ltd, 1948

Pencil, green, blue and black crayon, coloured washes and Chinese white (350 × 640), detail

Nicholson died during the final design stage of this project; it was completed by Hugh Casson and Neville Conder and opened in 1951. On a large site in the Buckinghamshire countryside, the Cement and Concrete Association created an experimental station. Architects from around the world came to inspect new forms, methods and finishes. The Structures Laboratory, one of the earliest and most costly buildings at the station, was appropriately made of concrete and used for testing the material's structural endurance. The open expanse of the interior covered 6,000 square feet and had 263 anchoring points in the pre-stressed floor. Wexham Springs closed in the early 1990s and Nicholson's only post-war building was demolished in 1995. This drawing is in Nicholson's hand.

447

76. Preliminary design for a radiogram, model 447, for Ferranti Ltd, 1946
Pencil and coloured crayon on tracing paper (385 × 430)

This radiogram, a unit combining a radio and record player, was manufactured by Ferranti to Nicholson's modified design. The walnut-veneered chassis remained similar in shape, but the plastic tuning knobs were aligned horizontally with the speaker and the storage for records more conveniently placed under the lid beside the turntable. And, more importantly in terms of aesthetics, the bentwood legs were abandoned in favour of splayed tapered struts that looked forward to the fifties rather than back to the thirties.

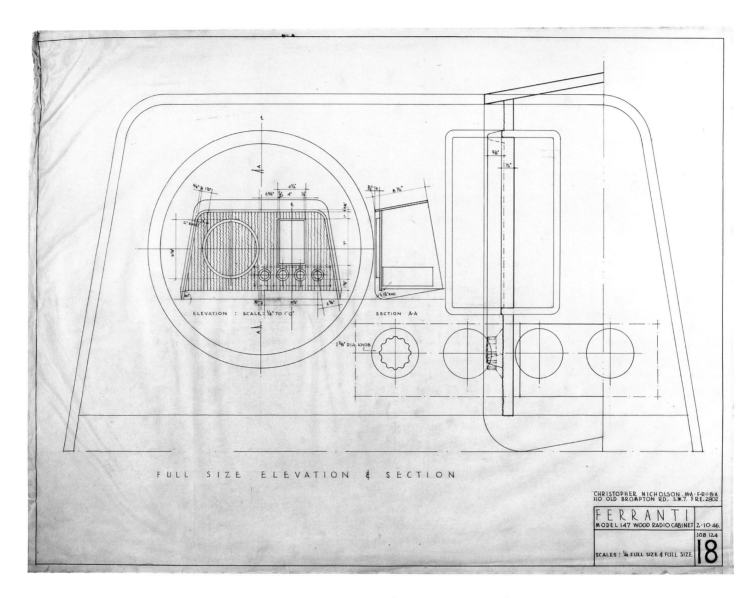

CHRISTOPHER NICHOLSON MA·F·R·I·B·A
110 OLD BROMPTON RD. S.W.7. FRE.2802

FERRANTI
MODEL 147 WOOD RADIO CABINET 2·10·46.

JOB 124

SCALES : ¼ FULL SIZE & FULL SIZE.

18

FULL SIZE ELEVATION & SECTION

77. Design for a radio, model 147, for Ferranti Ltd, 1946

Black and red pen and pencil on tracing paper (520 × 705)

This is a very clever drawing, showing the elevation full-size, overlaid at the right with a section, and then a reduced elevation placed in the circle of the speaker. Nicholson created many preliminary designs for his radios and televisions, varying the placement of the knobs, dial and speakers, and subtly reshaping the cabinet bodies. The 147 did go into production.

78. Design for a radio, model 248, for Ferranti Ltd, 1947
Pencil, coloured crayon and Chinese white (245 × 310)

New radio models came out annually, and this is Nicholson's updated version of his 147 from the previous year. When it went into production, the speaker and dial were reversed. The more boxy shape and wood casing is not as elegant as the earlier model's curvaceous line and cloth front. This may well be in response to the best-selling Murphy radios designed by the furniture-maker Gordon Russell. Nicholson's designs often anticipated new trends, and were not always fully appreciated in the conservative English market. Nicholson enjoyed drawing such perspectives as this one when he was ready to show his design to Ferranti.

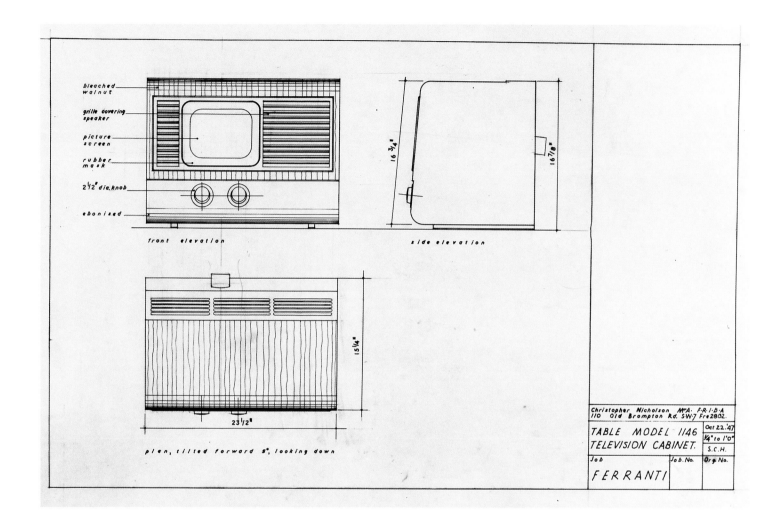

Labels on the drawing:

bleached walnut

grille covering speaker

picture screen

rubber mask

2½" dia. knob

ebonised

front elevation

side elevation

16 ¾"

16 ⅞"

15 ¼"

23½"

plan, tilted forward 5°, looking down

Christopher Nicholson M·A· F·R·I·B·A
110 Old Brompton Rd. S·W·7 Fre 2802.

TABLE MODEL 1146
TELEVISION CABINET.

Oct. 22. '47
¼" to 1'0"
S.C.H.

Job   Job. No.   Org No.

FERRANTI

79. Design for a television set, table model 1146, for Ferranti Ltd, 1947

Pen and pencil on tracing paper (370 × 565)

Nicholson first created a prototype of this small television set for his office display in the 1946 'Britain Can Make It' exhibition (plate 52). Neat and compact, with only a nine-inch screen, the set could be comfortably placed on a shelf like a radio. And because it did not dominate a room as did the larger, furniture-like models that were almost always symmetrical in design, Nicholson arranged the front of this set with the elements off-centre. The 1146 model did go into production, but not in large numbers; Ferranti was a small company and the market was restricted to viewers who lived within the limited range of the broadcasting centre at Alexandra Palace in North London. The price was also restricting – a television set was a luxury item.

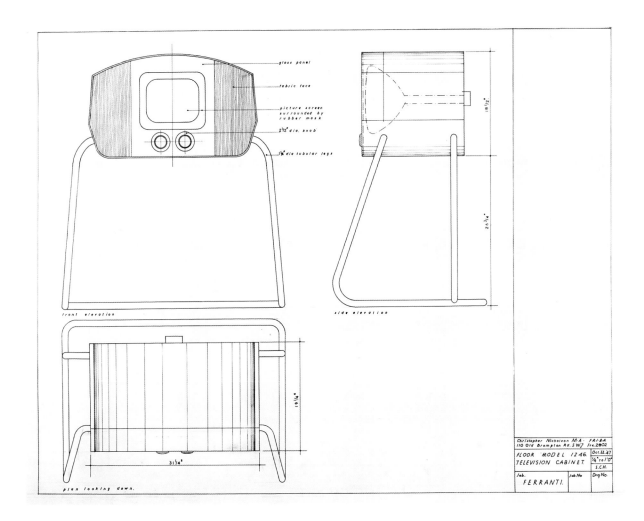

glass panel

fabric face

picture screen
surrounded by
rubber mask

2½" dia. knob

1¼" dia tubular legs

18½"

26¾"

front elevation

side elevation

19¼"

31¼"

plan looking down.

Christopher Nicholson M·A· F·R·I·B·A
110 Old Brompton Rd. S W7 Fre.2802
FLOOR MODEL 1246   Oct. 22. 47
TELEVISION CABINET   ¼" to 1'0"
                                    S.C.H.
Job.   Job No   Drg No.
FERRANTI.

80. Design for a television set, floor model 1246, for Ferranti Ltd, 1947

Pen and pencil on tracing paper (555 × 705)

This set, which was manufactured and sold, had the nickname of 'The Spider' at the Ferranti works in Manchester where it was made. Nicholson's pre-war experience of furniture design, especially his use of bent and moulded plywood and metals, came into play again in the late forties with his designs for radio and television cabinets, and as here with tubular legs. The 1246 chassis is metal, faced on the outer sides of the front with fabric and sheathed down the centre with toughened glass for added protection to the picture screen. There was always the worry that the tube might not only explode but implode.

ABOVE: Augustus John's studio, built in the garden of the artist's house, Fryern Court, Fordingbridge, Hampshire, 1935
BELOW: Interior of Augustus John's studio, 1935 (both photographs by Dell & Wainwright)

ABOVE: The south terrace front of Kit's Close, Fawley Green, Oxfordshire, 1938 (photographed by Dell & Wainwright);
BELOW: The entrance hall of Monkton House, Sussex, with the fish tank porthole on the staircase (photographed in 1986)

ABOVE: The garden landscape section of the MARS Group Exhibition, 1938, held at the New Burlington Galleries, London (photographed by Alfred Cracknell); *BELOW*: Nicholson's livery on a Vickers Viscount aeroplane and observation coach for British European Airways, *c*1947

CHRISTOPHER NICHOLSON: A CHRONOLOGY

1904   Christopher David George Nicholson, known familiarly as 'Kit', born on 16 December at 1 Pilgrim's Lane, Hampstead, London, the fourth and youngest child of the painters William Nicholson and Mabel Pryde

1906   Nicholson family moves to Mecklenburgh Square, London

1909   William Nicholson also acquires The Grange, Rottingdean, Sussex (sold 1914) and moves in London to The Vale, Chelsea

1916   Begins prep school at Heddon Court, East Barnet, Hertfordshire

1917   The family moves into 11 Apple Tree Yard, St James's

1918   Marriage of his sister Nancy to author and poet Robert Graves in January; deaths of his mother in July during influenza epidemic and brother Anthony in October of wounds in France

1919   Accepted to Gresham's School, Holt, Norfolk; his father marries Edith Stuart Wortley in October and the following year they have a daughter, Eliza, Christopher's half-sister

1920   Wedding of brother Ben to Winifred Roberts, also an artist, who purchase a villa at Castagnola, Italy, overlooking Lake Lugano. Christopher visits them some time during their two year stay

1923   Ben and Winifred Nicholson purchase Banks Head, Cumbria, to which Christopher makes frequent visits during the 1920s

1923-26   At Jesus College, Cambridge. Enrolled at Cambridge University School of Architecture

1926-27   Studies architecture at Princeton University, USA, having been awarded the Davison Scholarship

1928   First job designing a garden house, Boothby, Brampton, Cumbria, for Charles Roberts (plate 2); Carlisle Memorial, Brampton, Cumbria (plate 3)

1929   Returns to Cambridge in February to help Harold Tomlinson on a cinema competition design. In April, begins teaching first year students in the School of Architecture. Moves to 3 Malcolm Street, and about October 1930 to 13A Ram Yard

1931   Marries EQ Myers; begins alterations and additions to Hatherop Castle, Gloucestershire, for Sir Thomas Bazley, including entrance gates, squash court, fireplaces (plate 4); his brother Ben begins seeing the sculptor Barbara Hepworth, whom he eventually marries in 1938

1932   About this time worked for a short period with the architects Val Myer & Watson-Hart

1933   Rents top two floors of 100 Fulham Road as home and office; major alterations, 74 Elm Park Road, London, for R Blennerhassett (plates 7-9); about this time alters and designs interior of basement flat, 144A Sloane Street, London for the photographer JS Murray; begins studio at Fryern Court, Fordingbridge, Hampshire, for Augustus John (plates 10-12)

1934   Alterations to Durham Wharf, Chiswick Mall, London, for Julian Trevelyan (plate 17); furniture for Pioneer Health Centre, Peckham, London (plates 18-20)

1935   Hugh Casson joins office on a full-time basis as an assistant; terrace furniture for Messrs Heal & Son Ltd (plates 15-16); shopfront to 175 High Street North, Dunstable, for EAS Bernard; begins three of his most important commissions: alterations and additions for Monkton House, West Dean, Sussex, for Edward James (plates 21-22); Kit's Close, Fawley Green, Oxfordshire, for Dr Warren Crowe (plates 23-27); and the London Gliding Club, Dunstable, Bedfordshire (plates 33-39)

1936   Major commission for a house for Katia Freshfield, Dalingridge Farm, West Hoathly, Sussex (plates 29-30); alternative designs for headquarters buildings for the Royal Aeronautical Society in Boyle Street (plate 31) and Burlington Street, London; porch and entrance lobby to Fryern Court, Hampshire, for Augustus John; entrance porch to Quakers, Brasted Chart, Kent, for Antony MacNaughton; designs a house for Air Commodore BE Sutton at Halesend, Cradley, Herefordshire. This design is not built and instead he does alterations to his cottage (Quarry Cottage) the following year; first daughter, Jane, born; family moves to 29 Paultons Square, retaining 100 Fulham Road as the office

1937   Second daughter, Louisa Nancy, born; designs the garden landscape section MARS Group Exhibition of 1938 (plate 41); alterations to entrance hall of the Charterhouse Rheumatism Clinic, 56-60 Weymouth Street, London, for Dr Warren Crowe

1938   Competition design for a weekend cottage (plate 47); consulting room, 4 Upper Harley Street, London, for Mrs R Pritchard (plate 49); addition to the village hall, Aldingbourne, Sussex; design for the Pantheon, West Dean, West Sussex, for Edward James (plates 43-46)

1939   Designs airport for an article he co-authors on airport design in *Architect & Building News*; Nicholson's three major projects for the year not executed due to the outbreak of war: a house at Newnham-on-Severn, Gloucestershire for FAW Oliver; a glider factory, Icknield Way, Dunstable; and a staff canteen at Percival Aircraft Factory, Luton; joins the Royal Naval Volunteer Reserve, commissioned as a Lieutenant in the Fleet Air Arm; family moves to Hill Crest, near Southampton, Hampshire; elected Fellow of the RIBA; birth of son Timothy William

1941   Family moves to the Mill House, Fordingbridge, Hampshire

1945   Returns to civilian life and private practice, acquiring 110 Old Brompton Road as his office; teaches two terms at the Architectural Association

1946   Stand for 'Britain Can Make It' exhibition, Victoria & Albert Museum, London (plate 52); unexecuted design for house at Borough Green, Kent, for S Banks (plate 51); begins consultancy work for British European Airways which included ticket offices (in Paris, Glasgow & Stockholm), exhibition work, livery for aeroplanes and vehicles, and aeroplane interiors (plates 53-65 & 67); begins designing radio, radiogram and television chassis for Ferranti Ltd (plates 76-80); unexecuted design for Coln Hatherop & Quenington village centre, Gloucestershire (plate 66)

1947   Cargo freight exhibition stand, for BEA, BOAC & BSAA, Earl's Court, London (plate 68); exhibition stand for Ferranti, Radiolympia, London; alterations and additions to the Ward Room, HMS *Daedalus*, Lee-on-Solent, Hampshire (plate 72); designs civil air centre for Air Ministry committee (plates 73-74); family moves to West Blagdon Farm, near Cranborne, Dorset

1948   Elected to the Council of the Architectural Association; Ideal Home exhibition stand, for Arthur Sanderson & Sons, Olympia, London (plate 69); British Industries Fair exhibition stand for British Tube Investments, Birmingham (plate 70); British Industries Fair exhibition stand for Carnegie Chemicals (plate 71); designs the structures laboratory, Wexham Springs, Buckinghamshire, for the Cement and Concrete Association which is executed by Hugh Casson and Neville Conder (plate 75); dies 28 July in Italy

INDEX